GENESIS 34–50

Jacob and Egypt

John MacArthur

THOMAS NELSON

Since 1798

MacArthur Bible Studies

Genesis 34–50: Jacob and Egypt

© 2015 by John MacArthur

Published in Nashville, Tennessee, by Nelson Books, an imprint of Thomas Nelson. Nelson Books and Thomas Nelson are registered trademarks of HarperCollins Christian Publishing, Inc.

Originally published in association with the literary agency of Wolgemuth & Associates, Inc. Original layout, design, and writing assistance by Gregory C. Benoit Publishing, Old Mystic, Connecticut.

"Unleashing God's Truth, One Verse at a Time™" is a trademark of Grace to You. All rights reserved.

Thomas Nelson titles may be purchased in bulk for educational, business, fundraising, or sales promotional use. For information, please e-mail SpecialMarkets@ThomasNelson.com.

ISBN 978-0-7180-3457-3

First Printing December 2015 / Printed in the United States of America
HB 03.22.2024

CONTENTS

INTRODUCTION

Jacob, also called Israel, had twelve sons and one daughter. The book of Genesis gives us many vignettes from the lives of these people. Each was a very real human being, made of the same flesh as you and me, and with similar strengths and weaknesses. They each faced unique trials and temptations. One was raped, another was sold into slavery, and yet another was faced with the death of two sons.

Some of these characters responded by trusting in God's faithfulness alone, while others took revenge into their own hands. But one lesson emerges from all their stories: God was in control of all things! Even when it seemed He was nowhere to be found, He was, in fact, carefully guiding the events in these characters' lives. They did, after all, become the mighty nation of Israel.

This does not mean they lived *sinless* lives—quite the opposite, in some cases. Nevertheless, God was at work in them—even when they were living in sin—to bring about His plans for His people. What were His plans? Reconciliation in the family of Jacob—and in the lives of His people throughout the ages. For it was through Jacob's family that Christ was born.

In these twelve studies, we will examine the biblical events depicted in Genesis 34–50. We will look at Joseph's example of a servant and study how he became the model of a godly leader. We will witness Judah grow from a self-serving sinner into a qualified leader in his family. And, best of all, we will learn some precious truths about the character of God and see His great faithfulness in keeping His promises. We will learn, in short, what it means to walk by faith.

TITLE

The English title "Genesis" comes from the Septuagint (the Greek translation of the Bible) meaning "origins." Genesis serves to introduce the Pentateuch (the first five books of the Old Testament) and the entire Bible. The influence of Genesis in Scripture is demonstrated by the fact that it is quoted more than 35 times in the New Testament, with hundreds of allusions appearing in both Testaments. The story line of salvation, which begins in Genesis 3, is not completed until Revelation 21–22, where the eternal kingdom of redeemed believers is gloriously pictured.

AUTHOR AND DATE

While (1) the author does not identify himself in Genesis and (2) Genesis ends almost three centuries before Moses was born, both the Old Testament and the New Testament ascribe this composition to Moses (see, e.g., Exodus 17:14; Numbers 33:2; Ezra 6:18; Nehemiah 13:1; Matthew 8:4; Mark 12:26; Luke 16:29; John 5:46). Moses is the fitting author in light of his educational background (see Acts 7:22), and no compelling reasons have been forthcoming to challenge his authorship. Genesis was written after the Exodus (c. 1445 BC) but before Moses' death (c. 1405 BC).

BACKGROUND AND SETTING

The initial setting for Genesis is eternity past. God, by willful act and divine Word, spoke all creation into existence, furnished it, and breathed life into a lump of dirt that He fashioned in His image to become Adam. God made mankind the crowning point of His creation; i.e., His companions who would enjoy fellowship with Him and bring glory to His name.

The historical background for the early events in Genesis is clearly Mesopotamian. While it is difficult to pinpoint precisely the historical moment for which this book was written, Israel first heard Genesis sometime prior to crossing the Jordan River and entering the Promised Land (c. 1405 BC).

Genesis has three distinct sequential geographical settings: (1) Mesopotamia (chapters 1–11); (2) the Promised Land (chapters 12–36); and (3) Egypt (chapters 37–50). The time frames of these three segments are: (1) Creation to

c. 2090 BC; (2) 2090–1897 BC; and (3) 1897–1804 BC. Genesis covers more time than the remaining books of the Bible combined.

HISTORICAL AND THEOLOGICAL THEMES

In this book of beginnings, God revealed Himself and a worldview to Israel that contrasted, at times sharply, with the worldview of Israel's neighbors. The author made no attempt to defend the existence of God or to present a systematic discussion of His person and works. Rather, Israel's God distinguished Himself clearly from the alleged gods of her neighbors. Theological foundations are revealed, which include God the Father, God the Son, God the Holy Spirit, man, sin, redemption, covenant, promise, Satan and angels, kingdom, revelation, Israel, judgment, and blessing.

Genesis 1–11 (primeval history) reveals the origins of the universe; i.e., the beginnings of time and space and many of the firsts in human experience, such as marriage, family, the Fall, sin, redemption, judgment, and nations. Genesis 12–50 (patriarchal history) explained to Israel how they came into existence as a family whose ancestry could be traced to Eber (hence the "Hebrews"; see Genesis 10:24–25) and even more remotely to Shem, the son of Noah (hence the "Semites"; see Genesis 10:21). God's people came to understand not only their ancestry and family history but also the origins of their institutions, customs, languages, and different cultures, especially basic human experiences such as sin and death.

Because they were preparing to enter Canaan and dispossess the Canaanite inhabitants of their homes and properties, God revealed their enemies' background. In addition, they needed to understand the actual basis of the war they were about to declare in light of the immorality of killing, consistent with the other four books that Moses was writing (Exodus, Leviticus, Numbers, and Deuteronomy). Ultimately, the Jewish nation would understand a selected portion of preceding world history and the inaugural background of Israel as a basis by which they would live in their new beginnings under Joshua's leadership in the land that had previously been promised to Abraham, their original patriarchal forefather.

Genesis 12:1–3 established a primary focus on God's promises to Abraham. This narrowed their view from the entire world of peoples in Genesis 1–11 to one small nation, Israel, through whom God would progressively accomplish

His redemptive plan. This underscored Israel's mission to be "a light to the Gentiles" (Isaiah 42:6). God promised land, descendants (seed), and blessing. This threefold promise became, in turn, the basis of the covenant with Abraham (see Genesis 15:1–20). The rest of Scripture bears out the fulfillment of these promises.

On a larger scale, Genesis 1–11 set forth a singular message about the character and works of God. In the sequence of accounts which make up these chapters of Scripture, a pattern emerges that reveals God's abundant grace as He responded to the willful disobedience of mankind. Without exception, in each account God increased the manifestation of His grace. But also without exception, man responded in greater sinful rebellion. In biblical words, the more sin abounded, the more did God's grace abound (see Romans 5:20).

One final theme of both theological and historical significance that sets Genesis apart from other books of Scripture is that this first book of Scripture corresponds closely with the final book. In the book of Revelation, the paradise that was lost in Genesis will be regained. The apostle John clearly presented the events recorded in his book as future resolutions to the problems that began as a result of the curse in Genesis 3. His focus is on the effects of the Fall in the undoing of creation and the manner in which God rids His creation of the curse effect. In John's own words, "And there shall be no more curse" (Revelation 22:3). Not surprisingly, in the final chapter of God's Word, believers will find themselves back in the Garden of Eden, the eternal paradise of God, eating from the tree of life (see Revelation 22:1–14). At that time they will partake, wearing robes washed in the blood of the Lamb.

INTERPRETIVE CHALLENGES

Grasping the individual messages of Genesis that make up the larger plan and purpose of the book presents no small challenge, because both the individual accounts and the book's overall message offer important lessons to faith and works. Genesis presents creation by divine fiat, *ex nihilo*; i.e., "out of nothing." Three traumatic events of epic proportions—namely the Fall, the universal flood, and the dispersion of nations—are presented as historical backdrop in order to understand world history. From Abraham on, the pattern is to focus on God's redemption and blessing.

The customs of Genesis often differ considerably from those of our modern day. They must be explained against their ancient Near Eastern background. Each custom must also be treated according to the immediate context of the passage before any attempt is made to explain it based on customs recorded in extrabiblical sources or even elsewhere in Scripture.

JACOB AND EGYPT

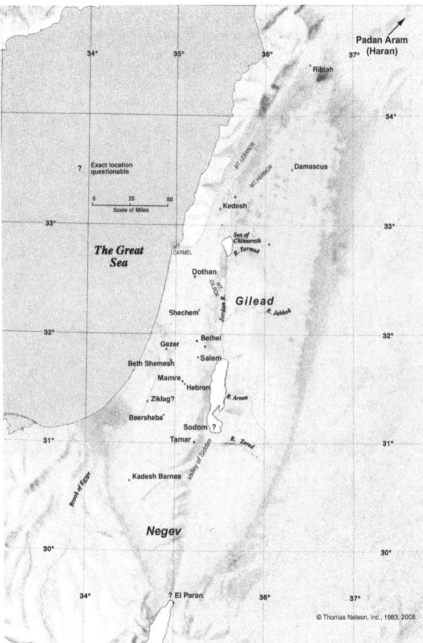

Padan Aram (Haran)

Riblah

34°

35°

36°

37°

34°

? Exact location questionable

MT. LEBANON

MT. HERMON

Damascus

0   25   50
Scale of Miles

Kedesh

33°

33°

The Great Sea

MT. CARMEL

Sea of Chinnereth

R. Yarmut

Dothan

MT. GILBOA

Jordan R.

Gilead

R. Jabbok

Shechem

32°

Bethel

Gezer

Salem

Beth Shemesh

Mamre

Hebron

R. Arnon

Ziklag?

Beersheba

Sodom ?

Tamar

R. Zered

31°

Valley of Siddim

Kadesh Barnea

Brook of Egypt

Negev

30°

30°

34°

? El Paran

36°

37°

© Thomas Nelson, Inc., 1983, 2008

THE DAUGHTER OF JACOB

Genesis 33:18–34:31

DRAWING NEAR

Jacob had a large family, with twelve sons and one daughter. What are some of the challenges that come with being in a family that has many brothers and sisters?

_____

_____

_____

THE CONTEXT

Our study opens with Jacob and his family living in Canaan at Shechem (see the map in the Introduction), where Jacob had journeyed after reconciling with his twin brother, Esau. By this time Jacob, also called Israel, had lived there for several years, and he had even purchased a parcel of land to live on. This was the first time that a descendant of Abraham had purchased land in Canaan, as far as we are told in Genesis, and it suggests that Jacob was settling down in Canaan.

Jacob, as you will recall, had two wives and two concubines. He had spent many years working for his uncle Laban, and during that time had fallen in love with Laban's younger daughter, Rachel. He had asked Laban for permission to marry Rachel, and Laban had agreed on one condition: Jacob would work for seven years to earn her hand. Jacob readily agreed to this condition, but at the end of the seven years, Laban tricked him by giving him his older daughter, Leah, instead of Rachel. Jacob then worked for another seven years to earn the hand of Rachel.

As time went on, Jacob loved Rachel more than Leah and made no effort to disguise the fact. This must have caused Leah deep grief, but the Lord comforted her by giving her six sons, while Rachel remained barren. Rachel, in turn, became jealous of her sister's fertility, and she persuaded Jacob to produce children through her maidservant. (The maidservant's children would have been viewed as being Rachel's.) Leah responded as though it were a competition, and she gave Jacob *her* maidservant. This competition continued between the two sisters, and Leah had another two sons and a daughter in the process—while Rachel had none.

Rachel eventually cried out to the Lord in her grief, and He showed His mercy and opened her womb. She gave birth to Joseph and later to Benjamin. Jacob eventually had a total of twelve sons, as well as at least one daughter. We will meet Jacob's twelve sons in the next study, but for now we will look at his daughter, Dinah. Dinah was the youngest of Leah's children, and she was probably between the ages of fourteen to sixteen at the time our passage opens.

In Jacob's day, it would have been unusual for a teenage girl to go wandering alone about the streets of a strange city. Yet this evidently is precisely what Dinah was about to do. We are not told the reasons for her excursion, but, as we shall see, the results would be quite dramatic.

KEYS TO THE TEXT

Read Genesis 33:18–34:31, noting the key words and phrases indicated below.

> JACOB IN CANAAN: *After reconciling with his brother, Jacob takes his family to Succoth and then settles near the city of Shechem in the land of Canaan.*

33:18. CAME SAFELY: This statement refers to the fulfillment of Jacob's vow made at Bethel when, after departing from Canaan, he looked to God for a safe return. Previously, Jacob had pledged to give a tithe (one-tenth of his possessions) back to God on arriving in Canaan (see Genesis 28:20–22). Presumably, he fulfilled this pledge at Shechem or, later, at Bethel (see 35:1).

19. BOUGHT THE PARCEL OF LAND WHERE HE HAD PITCHED HIS TENT: This purchase became only the second piece of real estate legally belonging to Abraham's line in the Promised Land (see Genesis 23:17–18; 25:9–10). However, the land was not Abraham's and his descendants simply because they bought it but, rather, because God owned it all (see Leviticus 25:23) and gave it to them for their exclusive domain.

20. ERECTED AN ALTAR: Jacob built an altar in the place where Abraham had previously erected one (see Genesis 12:6–7) and marked the spot with a new name: *El Elohe Israel,* which means "God, the God of Israel." In this way, Jacob declared that he worshiped the "Mighty One." The word *Israel* perhaps foreshadowed its use for the nation with which it rapidly became associated, even when it consisted of not much more than Jacob's extended household.

DINAH GOES OUT: So it is that Jacob purchases land in Shechem and settles his family there. One day, his daughter, Dinah, decides to go exploring on her own.

34:1. DINAH: Dinah was the eleventh child in Jacob's family, born to Leah after her sixth son, Zebulun (see Genesis 30:20–21).

WENT OUT TO SEE THE DAUGHTERS OF THE LAND: The meaning of this phrase is uncertain. Josephus, the Jewish historian, claimed this event occurred during a Canaanite festival and that Dinah went to see the women's finery. Apparently she went by herself, which would have been unusual in that culture. Ordinarily, a young woman would have been accompanied at least by her mother and female servants, and most likely also by her brothers. It is quite possible, then, that Dinah sneaked away without her father's consent.

2. SHECHEM: The city in which Jacob and his family were living was evidently also a family name within the tribe of Canaanites who lived there. Places frequently took their names from the tribe or leader who settled there. In this case, Shechem was the son of the region's ruler. The fact that Jacob had purchased a piece of land from Shechem suggests that he was planning on settling there. This was not God's plan, however, and Jacob's decision to settle with the Canaanites led to evil consequences.

TRAGEDY STRIKES: Young Dinah was not protected by her brothers, who were tending their flocks in the fields. A wealthy young ruler took advantage of her vulnerability.

SAW HER . . . TOOK HER . . . LAY WITH HER . . . VIOLATED HER: This is a profound picture of the cycle of sin. Shechem indulged the desire of his eyes, then reached out and took what he lusted after (as Eve did in Genesis 3), and then committed sin. This sin brought forth death, as it always does: "Each one is tempted when he is drawn away by his own desires and enticed. Then, when desire has conceived, it gives birth to sin; and sin, when it is full-grown, brings forth death" (James 1:14–15).

3. STRONGLY ATTRACTED: This phrase is a single Hebrew word meaning "to cling to" or "to be joined with." It is the same word translated *joined* in Genesis 2:24: "Therefore a man shall leave his father and mother and be joined to his wife, and they shall become one flesh." Despite the violence of Shechem's crime, he joined his soul with Dinah's.

HE LOVED THE YOUNG WOMAN: Shechem's sin was not undone or made right by his subsequent love toward Dinah. The same is true today. Neither is sin atoned for by our regrets, or even by our attempts to "make it up" to someone we have injured.

4. GET ME THIS YOUNG WOMAN AS A WIFE: This is actually quite close to God's law given through Moses: "If a man finds a young woman who is a virgin, who is not betrothed, and he seizes her and lies with her, and they are found out, then the man who lay with her shall give to the young woman's father fifty shekels of silver, and she shall be his wife because he has humbled her; he shall not be permitted to divorce her all his days" (Deuteronomy 22:28–29).

5. HE HAD DEFILED DINAH: The word *defile* means "to soil or pollute, to corrupt morally, or to make unfit for holy purposes." This is a serious concept, and it underscores the importance of sexual purity in God's people. Shechem had stolen something precious from Dinah and had corrupted her in the process.

JACOB HELD HIS PEACE UNTIL THEY CAME: Some have suggested that Jacob was looking to his sons for guidance in this matter. However, his reticence may simply have been the course of wisdom, whereby he sought counsel and took his time before reacting. Still, Jacob himself should have exerted godly leadership in this situation. His sons' subsequent actions suggest he was not a strong leader in his own household.

7. THE SONS OF JACOB CAME IN FROM THE FIELD WHEN THEY HEARD IT: The brothers' initial response to this crime was proper: they dropped what they were doing and rushed to help. God's people today should be equally quick to draw together when a brother or sister is in difficulties.

HE HAD DONE A DISGRACEFUL THING: Sexual immorality has become so common in our culture that Christians are prone to turn a blind eye to it. But this is not the way God sees promiscuity: in His eyes, sexual intercourse outside the bounds of marriage is a grave wickedness. It is a disgraceful thing when God's people fail to keep themselves sexually pure—it is "a thing which ought not to be done" (verse 7).

> SHECHEM REPENTS: *The young prince Shechem has committed a terrible crime against Dinah, but he quickly repents and tries to make restitution.*

8. GIVE HER TO HIM AS A WIFE: On the surface this was a reasonable request from Hamor, the father of Shechem, and it was in keeping with God's law. Dinah's honor had been violated, and it would have been difficult for her to find a husband in the future. The problem, however, was that the Canaanites did not serve God, and the people of Israel were not to intermarry with the world around them. It is understandable that Jacob was hesitant to make a decision here, as he was in a difficult position.

9. MAKE MARRIAGES WITH US: Abraham and Isaac had charged their sons not to take wives from among the Canaanites (see Genesis 24; 28:1), and Jacob understood this principle. God's people are not to intermarry with those who do not serve Him, because it is similar to yoking together an ox and a donkey: the two animals are completely different and will attempt to plow in different directions. "Do not be unequally yoked together with unbelievers. For what fellowship has righteousness with lawlessness? And what communion has light with darkness?" (2 Corinthians 6:14).

10. THE LAND SHALL BE BEFORE YOU: Hamor's offer was perfectly legitimate, even generous: "Settle with us; trade with us; become one of us; own land and homes." But the Lord had already promised the land to Abraham's

descendants, so from God's perspective it wasn't Hamor's to give. The Lord intended for His people to live as pilgrims and strangers in the land during Jacob's day (see Hebrews 11:9–10), and it was not time yet for the nation of Israel to settle into Canaan.

11. LET ME FIND FAVOR IN YOUR EYES: Shechem was asking for forgiveness, and he made it clear he was willing to make whatever restitution for his crime that Dinah's family demanded. His crime was grievous, but his sorrow seemed genuine. Shechem's behavior here was honorable.

THE BROTHERS CONSPIRE: Jacob's sons are unwilling to accept Shechem's offer of restitution. Instead, they plot to get revenge.

13. THE SONS OF JACOB . . . SPOKE DECEITFULLY: Jacob's life had been characterized by deceit and craftiness, and now his sons were following in his footsteps.

BECAUSE HE HAD DEFILED DINAH THEIR SISTER: There is no question that Shechem's violence toward Dinah was wicked, but all sin is wicked in the eyes of God. The young man had repented of his sin and expressed a desired to make whatever restitution was required. But the brothers responded with wickedness of their own.

14. WE CANNOT . . . GIVE OUR SISTER TO ONE WHO IS UNCIRCUMCISED: This statement from Jacob's sons was actually true, as the Lord did not want His people to intermarry with the Canaanites. But the Mosaic Law (which had not yet been given) made provisions for Gentiles to be circumcised and sojourn with God's people. The Lord's reason for selecting a chosen people in the first place was to make His grace evident to the entire world—not to simply bless the descendants of Abraham. Jacob's sons were grossly misusing God's provisions of grace to serve their own ends of revenge. "My beloved brethren, let every man be . . . slow to wrath; for the wrath of man does not produce the righteousness of God" (James 1:19–20).

THAT WOULD BE A REPROACH TO US: Ironically, what the sons of Jacob were about to do would also be a great reproach to them.

15. IF YOU WILL BECOME AS WE ARE: Here again we find an ironic statement, as Shechem was the one who was being honorable in this conversation, while the sons of Jacob were acting dishonorably.

16. WE WILL BECOME ONE PEOPLE: This remark from Jacob's sons was an outright lie. As Paul wrote, "Therefore, putting away lying, 'Let each one of you speak truth with his neighbor,' for we are members of one another" (Ephesians 4:25).

19. THE YOUNG MAN DID NOT DELAY: This proved Shechem's words were genuine, as he did not delay to do what Dinah's family required in making amends for his sin.

HE WAS MORE HONORABLE THAN ALL THE HOUSEHOLD OF HIS FATHER: This can be taken two ways. It indicates that Shechem was held in high esteem by his countrymen, as demonstrated by the fact that the men of the city submitted themselves to the painful and debilitating rite of circumcision. It also means that Shechem's actions, at least in part, were motivated by a genuine sorrow, while the actions of his father's household apparently were motivated by a desire for financial gain.

23. WILL NOT THEIR . . . PROPERTY . . . BE OURS: This seems to suggest that Hamor and Shechem were at least slightly motivated by the prospect of financial gain.

OVERKILL: *Jacob's sons take matters into their own hands and go far beyond justice in carrying out their vengeance.*

24. EVERY MALE WAS CIRCUMCISED: God made the covenant of circumcision with Abraham (see Genesis 17:9–13) as an outward sign that his household and descendants had cut off the flesh and entered into a new relationship of peace with the Lord. The rite was to be carried out when a boy was only eight days old, though it also permitted circumcision of adult men. Circumcision of an adult, however, was painful and incapacitating—as Jacob's sons were well aware. They were not interested in seeing the Canaanites make a covenant of peace with God; rather, they were concerned with satisfying their own lust for revenge.

25. SIMEON AND LEVI: Simeon and Levi were the second and third sons of Jacob. In the next study we will discuss how Jacob's firstborn son, Reuben, committed a gross sin that made him unfit to receive the birthright of the firstborn, but this sin by Simeon and Levi may be part of the reason why they also did not receive the birthright. That honor would eventually be passed to Judah,

who was fourth in line. Jesus was born through the line of Judah—not through Reuben, Simeon, or Levi.

26. THEY KILLED HAMOR AND SHECHEM: The punishment required by Mosaic Law was for Shechem to make restitution and marry the woman he had violated—not for the young man's death, and certainly not for the death of his family. Yet Jacob's sons went beyond even that extremity and slaughtered all the men of the city. This was nothing but the indulgence of bloodlust, and there was no justice in it.

27. THE SONS OF JACOB: Simeon and Levi were guilty of murder, but all the sons apparently took a share in the guilt by plundering the dead. This sad perversion of family unity would repeat itself when the brothers united together to murder Joseph.

30. THEY WILL GATHER THEMSELVES TOGETHER AGAINST ME AND KILL ME: Jacob's primary concern was his own safety, not the people who were slain or the wicked behavior of his sons. The sad irony is that Jacob would not have been faced with this danger if he had avoided settling in Shechem in the first place.

31. SHOULD HE TREAT OUR SISTER LIKE A HARLOT: The sons of Jacob were trying to justify their wickedness, but Shechem's honorable attempts at restitution point accusingly at their guilt. In the long run, Shechem had *not* treated Dinah like a harlot.

UNLEASHING THE TEXT

1) What motivated Dinah to go into town on her own? Do you think her actions were justified or unwise? Why?

_____

_____

_____

_____

_____

2) What motivated Dinah's brothers to carry out such a bloody revenge?
   If you had been in their place, what would you have done?

_____

_____

_____

3) Do you think Shechem's sorrow was genuine or insincere? Was his
   offer of marriage a sufficient recompense for what he had done?
   Support your answers from this passage.

_____

_____

_____

4) If you had been in Jacob's place, how would you have responded to
   Shechem's repentance?

_____

_____

_____

EXPLORING THE MEANING

God's people must live as pilgrims and strangers in this world. God had promised Abraham that his descendants would inherit the entire land of Canaan, but he himself was called to live like a nomad, moving from place to place without ever inheriting a single acre. The New Testament uses his example to teach us that Christians will inherit the eternal kingdom of God—but that kingdom is not of this world, and we must not lose sight of that fact.

Abraham "waited for the city which has foundations, whose builder and maker is God" (Hebrews 11:10), and his expectations were never realized in his lifetime. The same is true for God's people today: our true home is eternal, and the things of this world that consume our time and energies can distract us from storing up eternal treasures. Jacob lost sight of this when he bought land in Shechem and began to settle down.

It is not wrong to have a home and a career and to "put down roots" in a community. The danger lies in forgetting these things are only temporary. Our focus must always be on investing into the kingdom of God—investing for eternity rather than for today.

God hates sin, but He also forgives sin. Shechem was a lustful young man, and he lacked the discipline to control his passions. He saw a beautiful young girl, allowed his lust to control him, and defiled her. His sin brought shame both on himself and on an innocent girl—but then he repented of that sin and sought to make restitution.

In God's eyes, all sins are an absolute affront to his holy character—every act of disobedience, no matter how small and insignificant in our eyes, brings defilement and reproach on us and on others. But God, unlike Jacob's sons, also makes provision for repentance and restitution. What's more, He provides His Holy Spirit to believers in Jesus Christ, and the Spirit's role in part is to convict us of sin and urge us toward repentance.

Every one of us is guilty of wickedness, just as Shechem and Jacob's sons were guilty before God: "If we say that we have no sin, we deceive ourselves, and the truth is not in us" (1 John 1:8). But every one of us also has the opportunity to repent of sins and be fully restored to an unbroken relationship with our Creator: "If we confess our sins, He is faithful and just to forgive us our sins and to cleanse us from all unrighteousness" (verse 9).

Vengeance belongs to God, not to us. Shechem's sin against Dinah brought disgrace on her entire family, and her brothers were right to be angry. They were wrong, however, to take their own revenge on the people of that city. In so doing, they were as guilty as Shechem for not controlling their own passions.

We all suffer at the hands of other people from time to time, and sometimes we can be called to suffer greatly. However, we must remember to view such sufferings as God's tools of purification and strengthening for us. Those who hate us are not permitted to cause evil in our lives unless God allows it— and when He allows it, He does so for a reason.

God's reasons for allowing His children to suffer are always intended to bring glory to His name. It may be that He is working to bring the wrong-doer to salvation, or perhaps He is working on making us more like Christ. Whether we can see a reason or not, we must never repay evil with evil. "Beloved, do not avenge yourselves, but rather give place to wrath; for it is written, 'Vengeance is Mine, I will repay,' says the Lord. Therefore 'If your enemy is hungry, feed him; if he is thirsty, give him a drink; for in so doing you will heap coals of fire on his head.' Do not be overcome by evil, but overcome evil with good" (Romans 12:19–21).

God calls His people to be instruments of grace, not weapons of wrath. The Lord had instituted the covenant of circumcision with Abraham's descendants to provide an outward, visible sign to the world that the Israelites were His people. That covenant was for God's glory, not because Israel had done something to earn His favor. Jacob's sons, however, used God's provision of grace for their own lustful purposes, and in so doing they brought disgrace on God's name.

REFLECTING ON THE TEXT

5) In your opinion, what motivated Jacob to purchase land near Shechem? Was this wise or unwise? Why?

_____

_____

_____

_____

_____

_____

6) Have you ever known someone who committed a grievous sin but then later repented? What fruits of repentance (evidence of a changed heart) did that person exhibit in his or her life?

_____

_____

_____

_____

7) How should Jacob have responded to Shechem's sin? Did Jacob do the right thing regarding Shechem? Regarding his sons?

_____

_____

_____

_____

_____

8) When have you seen God's grace demonstrated by someone who was wronged? Is there a circumstance in your life right now in which you can demonstrate grace toward someone else?

_____

_____

_____

_____

PERSONAL RESPONSE

9) How do you respond when someone wrongs you? Do you take revenge or offer forgiveness?

_____

_____

_____

_____

_____

10) How do you respond when you have committed a sin against someone else? Do you seek forgiveness and offer restitution?

_____

_____

_____

_____

_____

2

The Sons of Jacob

Genesis 35:1–29; 37:1–36

Drawing Near

In this study, we will see how Joseph made the mistake of sharing too much information with his brothers. When have you done something similar that created problems for you?

_____

_____

_____

_____

The Context

When Jacob learned of what his sons had done in Shechem, he said to them, "You have troubled me by making me obnoxious among the inhabitants of the land . . . and since I am few in number, they will gather themselves together against me and kill me" (Genesis 34:30). Jacob knew the vengeance his sons had exacted would result in retaliation. His loss of respect among his neighbors and the end of their peaceful relations put both him and his family in harm's way. This imminent threat tested God's promise of safety and gave Jacob cause for great concern.

So God called Jacob to move from that place and settle in Bethel, where He had previously appeared to Jacob in a dream and confirmed with him the covenant that He had made with his grandfather Abraham (see Genesis 28:13–15). God would watch over and protect the family as they fled, and once again He would appear to Jacob in that place and confirm his new name, Israel. It would also be in Bethel that Rachel, Jacob's beloved wife, would die after giving birth to her second son, Benjamin.

As time moved on, Jacob began to take great delight in his sons born late in his life through Rachel. This led to him playing favorites among them, loving Joseph and Benjamin more openly than he did any of his other ten. Needless to say, Jacob's older sons came to resent this fact, and ultimately they would take it out on Joseph.

All of this favoritism and competition and resentment led to a household that lacked peace and unity. As our study opens, Jacob's sons are mostly grown men with families of their own, and Joseph is seventeen. The tensions among the brothers are about to come to a head.

KEYS TO THE TEXT

Read Genesis 35:1–29, noting the key words and phrases indicated below.

> RETURN TO BETHEL: *Jacob's move to Bethel requires not only logistical planning for the journey but also spiritual housecleaning in the form of getting rid of all idols.*

35:2. PUT AWAY THE FOREIGN GODS: It was no longer tolerable for Jacob's family to possess idolatrous symbols such as figurines, amulets, or cultic charms. Idols buried out of sight, plus bathing and changing to clean clothes, all served to portray both cleansing from defilement by idolatry and consecration of the heart to the Lord.

5. THE TERROR OF GOD: A supernaturally induced fear of Israel rendered the surrounding city-states unwilling and powerless to intervene and made Jacob's fear of their retaliation rather inconsequential.

7. BUILT AN ALTAR THERE: Jacob reconfirmed his allegiance to God through this act of worship. God, in turn, reaffirmed His commitment to Jacob by reappearing to him, repeating the change of his name, and rehearsing the Abrahamic promises.

11. KINGS SHALL COME FROM YOUR BODY: God's words, included here for the first time since His promises at Abraham's circumcision (see Genesis 17:6, 16), served as a reminder of future royalty.

13. WENT UP: The presence of God was there in some visible form.

16. EPHRATH: A more ancient name for Bethlehem.

18. BEN-ONI . . . BENJAMIN: Rachel appropriately named her newborn "son of my sorrow," but the grieving father named him "son of my right hand," thus assigning him a place of honor in the home.

My TWELVE SONS: The birth of Benjamin in Canaan furnishes reason to review the sons born outside of Canaan, with only one sad note preceding it.

22. REUBEN WENT AND LAY WITH BILHAH: Reuben was Jacob's oldest son, born through Leah, and Bilhah was Rachel's maidservant. This grievous sin cost Reuben his birthright and his status as firstborn.

23. LEVI: The descendants of Levi would eventually become the only men eligible for the priesthood in Israel.

JUDAH: David would be a descendant of Judah—and ultimately so would Jesus Himself. (We will look more closely at Judah in the next study.)

24. BENJAMIN: Jacob was more than one hundred years old when Benjamin, his last son, was born to Rachel.

26. PADAN ARAM: This region was many days to the northeast of where Isaac was living. It is also where Abraham was living when God called him to journey to Canaan.

27. MAMRE: This location was important in Abraham's life—such as when he met God face-to-face and interceded for Sodom and Gomorrah.

29. HIS SONS ESAU AND JACOB: Isaac's funeral brought his two sons together, as Abraham's funeral had done for Isaac and Ishmael (see Genesis 25:9).

Read Genesis 37:1–36, noting the key words and phrases indicated below.

TENSIONS BEGIN TO BUILD: Jacob not only plays favorites with his wives but also with his sons. This soon creates problems within his family.

1. WHERE HIS FATHER WAS A STRANGER: God had commanded Abraham, Jacob's grandfather, to move to Canaan so his descendants could inherit

the entire land. But Abraham himself had lived as a pilgrim in the land God had promised him and had died without actually seeing the fulfillment of God's promise. The same was true of Isaac and would eventually be the case for Jacob.

2. JOSEPH BROUGHT A BAD REPORT: We are not told whether this report was the result of Jacob's questioning his son or Joseph voluntarily bearing the report to his father. We also do not know what the report was about, so it is difficult to assess Joseph's actions here. Some have suggested that he was spiritually proud or self-righteous, but these conclusions are not supported by what we know. The important element of this verse is that Joseph's brothers resented him, and their resentment had reached the breaking point.

3. ISRAEL LOVED JOSEPH MORE THAN ALL HIS CHILDREN: There is a sad irony in this favoritism, because Jacob himself had grown up with parents who played favorites. This in part had led to the permanent separation of Jacob from his brother, Esau, and it would lead to division and attempted murder among his own children.

TUNIC OF MANY COLORS: The meaning of this phrase is uncertain—it may simply refer to a robe with long sleeves. Whatever its distinguishing features, this cloak signified Jacob's favoritism of Joseph (see 2 Samuel 13:18) and perhaps also some level of Joseph's authority over his brothers.

4. THEY HATED HIM: From a human perspective, this is the natural result of a father choosing favorites among his children. This animosity was also modeled by Rachel and Leah, for there was deep resentment and jealousy between them. Nevertheless, a person is never justified in the eyes of God when he hates his brothers.

THAT DREAMER OF DREAMS: God gives Joseph prophetic dreams concerning the future, but this only serves to increase his brothers' resentment.

5. JOSEPH HAD A DREAM: The dreams the Lord gave to Joseph predicted that he would one day rule over his entire family. This served merely to deepen his brothers' resentment. In their eyes, he was being presumptuous and arrogant.

7. MY SHEAF AROSE: Joseph's brothers needed no special interpretation to catch the meaning and significance of his dreams.

9. HE DREAMED STILL ANOTHER DREAM: It is important to note that Joseph had two dreams rather than one. In the first dream, his brothers bowed themselves before him; in the second, his entire family bowed. This would be fulfilled in the two stages of his family's move to Egypt. The Lord had every step planned out in advance, and the conspiracies of men could not prevent its fulfillment.

11. HIS BROTHERS ENVIED HIM: Here we are told the true motives behind the brothers' reaction: they envied God's plan for Joseph's life. A proper brotherly love toward Joseph would have prompted his family to rejoice in the Lord's favor toward him.

KEPT THE MATTER IN MIND: Jacob, notwithstanding his public admonishment of Joseph, continued to ponder the meaning of the dreams.

JEALOUSY REARS ITS UGLY HEAD: Joseph's brothers resent him and reject the idea that he will one day rule over them. Now they put their resentment into action.

12. SHECHEM: Located about fifty miles north of Mamre.

13. HERE I AM: Joseph demonstrated a submissive attitude throughout his life. He was always ready to obey his father, and would be equally loyal and submissive to his masters in Egypt. In this he pictures the obedience of Christ, who submitted Himself completely to the will of His Father in all things—even to death on the cross.

14. HEBRON: Located about fifty miles south of Shechem.

17. DOTHAN: Located almost fifteen miles north of Shechem.

18. THEY CONSPIRED AGAINST HIM TO KILL HIM: The brothers were carrying out the sin of Cain, who murdered his own brother because Abel's offering was acceptable to the Lord while Cain's was rejected. Jacob's sons had been stirred to hatred of their brother because of his prophetic dreams and their father's preference, so, as with Cain, this would have been premeditated murder, not accidental manslaughter or even a momentary passion. Jesus would later suffer in a similar manner: "Then, from that day on, they plotted to put Him to death" (John 11:53).

19. THIS DREAMER: The brothers revealed here that they deeply resented Joseph's dreams. It may well be that they resented God's favor toward Joseph in the same way as they resented Jacob's favoritism. Yet God's favor toward an individual has nothing in common with a parent's unfair favoritism, for God does not choose favorites. All men and women stand equal before Him, justified only by His Son's blood.

PLOTTING MURDER: Joseph goes out to find his brothers in the fields, but they see him coming and plot his death. However, one brother tries to save him.

20. LET US NOW KILL HIM: The sons of Jacob meant exactly what they said: it was their deliberate intention to murder their brother Joseph. We will see that God used their wicked plans for His good purposes, but we must not overlook the fact that Joseph's brothers fully intended to kill him.

WHAT WILL BECOME OF HIS DREAMS: Joseph's brothers had the same opportunities to serve God and be used by Him that Joseph had, but their own anger and resentment were getting in the way.

21. REUBEN: As we have seen, Reuben was Jacob's firstborn son and the rightful heir to the birthright, but he would eventually lose that birthright because of a grievous sin committed against his father (see Genesis 35:22). Nevertheless, at this point Reuben seemed to be taking his role as firstborn seriously, for he was the only one of the brothers who attempted to save Joseph's life.

23. THEY STRIPPED JOSEPH OF HIS TUNIC: The brothers' attitude was one of angry vengeance. They had already expressed their desire to prevent Joseph's prophetic dreams from coming to fulfillment, and now they hoped to spite their father's favoritism. There was also a grim pragmatism in this gesture, as they intended to use the tunic to hide their crime. This scene is hauntingly familiar to what would later happen to Christ: "Then they crucified Him, and divided His garments, casting lots, that it might be fulfilled which was spoken by the prophet: 'They divided My garments among them, and for My clothing they cast lots'" (Matthew 27:35).

24. CAST HIM INTO A PIT: There are interesting parallels between this experience and what Joseph will later suffer in Egypt, when Potiphar's wife strips him of his cloak and he is thrown into the pit of a prison.

SOLD INTO SLAVERY: Joseph's hard-hearted brothers have agreed not to murder him, but that does not mean they will let him return home. There is a more profitable way.

25. THEY SAT DOWN TO EAT A MEAL: What a picture of coldhearted ruthlessness! Joseph's brothers had set out to murder their own flesh and blood, yet their consciences did not bother them in the least. They were content to sit at the mouth of the pit and eat lunch, probably hearing the pleas of Joseph all the while. This callous behavior is reminiscent of those who stood at the foot of the cross and mocked the Savior: "He saved others; Himself He cannot save. If He is the King of Israel, let Him now come down from the cross, and we will believe Him" (Matthew 27:42).

A COMPANY OF ISHMAELITES: This caravan was composed of Midianites as well as Ishmaelites. The Midianites were descended from Abraham and Keturah (see Genesis 25:1–2), and the Ishmaelites were descended from Abraham and Hagar (see Genesis 16). These traders, therefore, were actually distant cousins of Joseph and his brothers.

26. WHAT PROFIT IS THERE: Judah's words seemed to indicate that the brothers were undecided about what to do with Joseph. Reuben intended to take Joseph safely home, but he had evidently gone off at this point to tend sheep. The remaining brothers still had no intention of taking Joseph home. It is sad that the closest they came to showing mercy was when it might bring a profit.

27. HE IS OUR BROTHER AND OUR FLESH: It is possible that Judah was sincerely trying to save Joseph's life, but it is equally possible that he was being self-righteous in this sentiment. Either way, he later came to recognize that he was as responsible as anyone for the treachery done to his flesh and blood.

28. SOLD HIM TO THE ISHMAELITES FOR TWENTY SHEKELS OF SILVER: In a similar manner, Judas would "sell" Jesus to the religious leaders for thirty pieces of silver (see Matthew 26:14–15; 27:9).

29. REUBEN RETURNED TO THE PIT: Reuben's intentions were good, but his leadership over his brothers proved ineffective because he had already lost his position in God's eyes. Interestingly, in contrast, Judah was already developing into the leader of his brothers—even though that leadership was toward evil at this point.

30. WHERE SHALL I GO: Reuben provides us with a good contrast to Judah in their respective responses. Reuben's response here was certainly one of grief and sorrow, yet the focus was still on himself. Judah would later respond to Benjamin's danger by worrying about its effect on his father.

31. KILLED A KID OF THE GOATS: This blood would deceive Jacob into believing that his beloved son was dead. Here we find another irony that dated back to Jacob's own life, when he killed a kid and used its skin to deceive his father, Isaac, into believing he was Esau (see Genesis 27).

UNLEASHING THE TEXT

1) Where did the competition and resentment originate among the twelve sons? Why did they hate Joseph in particular?

_____

_____

_____

2) What, if anything, did Joseph do to make his troubles worse? In what ways was he completely innocent?

_____

_____

_____

3) Put yourself in Joseph's place. What would you have been thinking as you sat at the bottom of the pit? How would you have responded to your brothers? To God?

_____

_____

_____

4) It was actually God's plan for Joseph to go into Egypt. What are some ways in which God was leading these events behind the scenes?

_____

_____

_____

EXPLORING THE MEANING

God is in control of all our circumstances, even when things seem to be going wrong. The Lord had told Abraham, many years before, that his descendants would go into Egypt for 400 years (see Genesis 15:13–14). As we will see in the upcoming studies, it was His plan from the beginning that Joseph should lead his family into Egypt. The events in these passages were part of that plan.

However, the hand of God was not readily apparent in these events, particularly to the people who were living through them. Joseph certainly did not sit rejoicing at the bottom of the pit, feeling delighted that God was sending him into Egypt to fulfill His prophecy to Abraham. It is much more likely that he was overcome with grief and fear, wondering what was going to happen next—wondering, indeed, if he would be murdered by his own brothers.

Yet the sovereign Lord retained control over Joseph's life. He is completely sovereign over all things in *our* lives too, and He has promised that He will always be faithful to His children. "And we know that all things work together for good to those who love God, to those who are the called according to His purpose" (Romans 8:28).

We are still responsible for our own actions. The other side to the previous principle is that God's sovereignty does not exonerate us from our own responsibility. Nor does it prevent others from attempting to do harm against us. As we have seen in this passage of Scripture, the brothers were fully responsible before God for attempting to murder Joseph and for selling him into slavery.

God's plans cannot be thwarted by the actions of human beings or even by Satan himself. So the Lord can—and does—use the wicked actions of evil men to accomplish His holy purposes. However, this is to the glory of God, not to the praise of wicked men. Joseph's brothers still had to answer for their deeds even though God used those actions to further His plans for Israel.

The good news is that the Lord also uses our obedience to further His purposes and bring glory to His name—and we grow in Christlikeness in the process. Joseph's responses to his brothers' deeds revealed this in his life, and he became a picture of the life of Christ.

Hatred and resentment lead to murder. Cain demonstrated this principle when he became resentful of his brother's favor with the Lord (see Genesis 4), finally taking it out in violence. Jacob's sons repeated this sin when they allowed their resentment to grow into hatred for Joseph.

We run the same risk when we allow bitterness and resentment to grow in us. We may never commit actual physical murder, but our resentment and hatred are equivalent: "Whoever hates his brother is a murderer, and you know that no murderer has eternal life abiding in him" (1 John 3:15). "If someone says, 'I love God,' and hates his brother, he is a liar; for he who does not love his brother whom he has seen, how can he love God whom he has not seen?" (1 John 4:20).

When we find resentment growing in us toward another person, we must recognize that it is ultimately directed against God. It is vital that we repent of these attitudes and submit ourselves to God's sovereignty, even when the circumstances may seem unjust.

REFLECTING ON THE TEXT

5) If there had been no hatred among the twelve sons, how might they have reacted differently to Joseph's dreams?

_____

_____

_____

_____

6) God wanted Joseph to go into Egypt for His own purposes. How do we balance the sovereignty of God with the sinful deeds of people?

_____

_____

_____

7) Why did the brothers resent Joseph's dreams? What does this reveal about the deeper levels of their anger and resentment?

_____

_____

_____

8) Why did God allow Joseph to suffer this mistreatment when he had done nothing to deserve it?

_____

_____

_____

PERSONAL RESPONSE

9) Are you struggling with resentment or anger toward another person? What will you do this week to forgive that person?

_____

_____

_____

10) What situations are you facing that seem out of control? How might
the Lord be using those situations for His own purposes?

_____

_____

_____

_____

3

JUDAH AND TAMAR

Genesis 38:1–29

DRAWING NEAR

Why is it so important for people to keep their commitments to one other? How does it affect a relationship if the people within it do not honor their word?

_____

_____

_____

THE CONTEXT

Joseph had been wrenched from his family against his will, but his brother Judah would now leave the family voluntarily in hopes of personal gain. Judah surrounded himself with Canaanite friends and even took a Canaanite wife. By doing so, he disregarded his family's injunctions against intermarriage.

Judah's move to Canaan highlights the danger that Israel faced: if left in Canaan, they might well have intermarried and drifted from God's special calling to be separated to Him. The Lord forced Jacob to move his family to Egypt in part to preserve them from that danger. Once there, the family had no choice but to live apart from the Egyptians, who did not want anything to do with them.

This interlude into Judah's life is bracketed on each side by references of the sale of Joseph to Potiphar (see Genesis 37:36; 39:1) and seems to interrupt the main narrative. Such a parenthesis demands some reason as to why a chapter laced with wickedness, immorality, and subterfuge should of necessity be placed in this spot. The answer is that the account fits the events chronologically, genealogically, and thematically.

The events recorded are chronologically in the right place, as they are contemporary with the time of Joseph's slavery in Egypt. The account is genealogically in the right place because now that Joseph was gone (seemingly for good), and with Reuben, Simeon, and Levi out of favor with their father (for incest and for treachery), Judah would most likely accede to firstborn status. The story is thematically in the right place because it provides a striking contrast between the immoral character of Judah and the virtue of Joseph.

As we will see in this study, though Judah was now in line to receive the rights of the firstborn, he, too, was unqualified to be the family's spiritual leader. Fortunately, God's grace overrides man's sin, and He can turn even human failures into His glory. God was at work in Judah's life to prepare him for his role as leader—and ultimately to bring His own Son into the world through Judah's descendants.

KEYS TO THE TEXT

Read Genesis 38:1–29, noting the key words and phrases indicated below.

> *JUDAH LEAVES HOME: Judah's decision to leave home is*
> *motivated by his own desire for personal gain. He turns his back not*
> *only on his family but also on God's teachings.*

38:1. AT THAT TIME: The events in this chapter took place around the time Joseph was sold into Egypt—perhaps while he was still in Potiphar's household. Joseph's response to Potiphar's wife would present a stark contrast to Judah's behavior in this chapter.

JUDAH DEPARTED FROM HIS BROTHERS: Judah evidently left his family altogether and moved to a nearby Canaanite town. He was effectively turning his back on the teaching of Abraham, Isaac, and Jacob. Here we see a distinction between himself and his brother Joseph, who had been separated from his family by force, while Judah did so of his own accord.

ADULLAMITE: Adullam was a town near Hebron.

PRESERVING A HERITAGE: Judah takes a Canaanite wife and then watches his sons die for their wickedness. He fears that his lineage will be cut off.

2. HE MARRIED HER: Abraham and Isaac had both made it clear to their sons that they were not to marry Canaanite women (see Genesis 24:3; 28:1), but Judah deliberately ignored the injunction.

6. JUDAH TOOK A WIFE FOR ER: We know little about Tamar, the woman whom Judah selected to marry his son, but it is likely that she was also a Canaanite. Had the Lord permitted the sons of Jacob to remain in Canaan, they would have become indistinguishable from the world around them within a few generations.

8. RAISE UP AN HEIR TO YOUR BROTHER: The Mosaic Law would later codify this practice, known as a levirate marriage. If a man died without an heir, his brother was expected to marry the widow and produce an heir for his dead brother (see Deuteronomy 25:5–10). This was what Judah was requesting of his son Onan, because Er had died for unspecified wickedness.

9. BUT ONAN KNEW THAT THE HEIR WOULD NOT BE HIS: According to the levirate marital practices, Onan's firstborn son would, in fact, take the name of Er and be considered Er's heir rather than Onan's.

HE EMITTED ON THE GROUND, LEST HE SHOULD GIVE AN HEIR TO HIS BROTHER: Onan's attitude was completely self-serving, and he refused to look after his late brother's heritage. His behavior is reminiscent of Cain, who insisted that he was not his "brother's keeper" (Genesis 4:9).

10. THEREFORE HE KILLED HIM ALSO: The Lord executed Onan due to his deliberate and rebellious rejection of his duty to marry a relative's widow. This was a rather dubious distinction for the line of Judah to gain.

11. LEST HE ALSO DIE LIKE HIS BROTHERS: Judah had now lost two sons during his sojourn in Canaan, and he would have no heir if he lost his third son, Shelah. So he told Er's widow to wait until this son grew up, knowing full well that Shelah would never marry her.

DWELT IN HER FATHER'S HOUSE: Tamar took her father-in-law at his word and remained in his household as a widow.

INDULGING THE FLESH: Some time later, Judah hires a prostitute. He doesn't know, however, that she is his own daughter-in-law.

12. TIMNAH: The specific location of this Canaanite city in the hill country of Judah is unknown, but it would also prove to be a snare to Samson, who took a Canaanite wife there (see Judges 14).

13. SHEAR HIS SHEEP: Sheep-shearing time was renowned in Canaanite culture for its festivities and licentious behavior. The pagan cultures worshiped many false gods and practiced fertility rites during sheep shearing and harvest.

14. COVERED HERSELF WITH A VEIL AND WRAPPED HERSELF: Tamar deliberately disguised herself as a prostitute, evidently intending to trap Judah. This suggests that she had little respect for Judah's character.

SHE WAS NOT GIVEN TO HIM AS A WIFE: Tamar had waited in vain for Judah to give his third son, Shelah, to her in marriage to protect the inheritance rights of her deceased husband. It was a disgrace in that culture for a woman to have no children, and the name and heritage of her first husband, Er, would be wiped out if she remained a childless widow. So Tamar took desperate measures and resorted to subterfuge to address the problem. In so doing, she may have been influenced by Hittite inheritance practices, which called the father-in-law into levirate marriage in the absence of sons to fulfill that duty.

16. PLEASE LET ME COME IN TO YOU: Judah demonstrated that Tamar's opinion of his moral character was correct, as he initiated the sin.

18. YOUR SIGNET AND CORD, AND YOUR STAFF: It was customary in that culture for people to require three forms of "identification" in ratifying a contract. The signet was probably a cylinder that Judah wore on a cord around his neck and was used to endorse legal documents. His staff was probably unique in some way, such that it was easily recognizable as his personal property.

23. LEST WE BE SHAMED: It would certainly not be good for Judah's reputation if he went about town asking the whereabouts of a local prostitute, so he dropped the issue. The sad irony is that his shameful deed would be found out far more dramatically than he anticipated.

I SENT THIS YOUNG GOAT: Judah may have thought that the shame of his action was in not paying the prostitute. He evidently felt that he had fulfilled his responsibility by making concerted efforts to pay her, and evidently he thought no more about it.

24. LET HER BE BURNED: Judah's hypocrisy is astounding here, as he demanded that his daughter-in-law be burned to death for prostituting herself, without giving any thought to his own apparent habit of hiring prostitutes himself. Mosaic legislation would later prescribe this form of the death penalty for a priest's daughter who prostituted herself or for those guilty of certain forms of incest (see Leviticus 20:14; 21:9).

26. SHE HAS BEEN MORE RIGHTEOUS THAN I: Judah was not endorsing Tamar's deeds but acknowledging that she had been attentive to proper inheritance rights, which he had blatantly ignored. He also was smitten with the confrontation of his own sinful behavior and recognized his hypocrisy. This may have been a turning point in Judah's life, for as we go along we will see that he becomes a responsible man.

29. PEREZ: Meaning "breach" or "pushing through." This first of Tamar's twins, born of prostitution and incest, nevertheless came into the messianic line that went through Boaz and Ruth to King David (see Ruth 4:18–22; Matthew 1:3). God, in His grace, can turn even our sinful acts to His glory.

GOING DEEPER

In 1 Corinthians 6:12–20, Paul discusses the importance for believers in Christ to abstain from sexually immoral acts like Judah committed. Read that passage and note the key words and phrases below.

> *THE CHRISTIAN'S RIGHTS: The Corinthian believers mistakenly believe that because they are free in Christ, they are free to sin. In this passage, Paul seeks to correct that error.*

6:12. ALL THINGS ARE LAWFUL: This might have been a Corinthian slogan. Paul needed to stress to the believers that while it is true that God forgives all sins, not everything they did was profitable or beneficial. The price of abusing freedom and grace was very high. Sin always produces loss.

POWER: The original Greek word means "mastered," and no sin is more enslaving than sexual sin. Sexual sin controls, so believers must never allow it to have that control. Instead, they must master sexual sin in the Lord's strength.

13. FOODS FOR THE STOMACH: Perhaps this was a popular proverb to celebrate the idea that sex is purely biological, like eating. The Corinthians, similar to many of their pagan friends, probably used that analogy to justify sexual immorality. Paul rejected this convenient justifying analogy.

14. WILL ALSO RAISE US: Paul here is referring to the believer's body being changed, raised, glorified, and made heavenly.

JOINED WITH CHRIST: Paul stresses that the believer's body is not only for the Lord in the here and now, but is of the Lord, a part of His body, the church.

15. BODIES ARE MEMBERS: The Christian's body is a temple in which the Spirit of Christ lives. Therefore, when a believer commits a sexual sin, it involves Christ with a harlot, or prostitute. All sexual sin is harlotry.

CERTAINLY NOT: These words translate the strongest Greek negative: "May it never be so."

16. ONE FLESH: Paul supports his point by appealing to the truth of Genesis 2:24, which defines the sexual union between a man and a woman as "one flesh." When a person is joined to a prostitute, it is a one-flesh experience. Therefore, Christ is spiritually joined to that harlot.

17. ONE SPIRIT WITH HIM: Further strengthening the point, Paul affirms that all sex outside of marriage is sin, but illicit relationships by believers are especially reprehensible because they profane Jesus Christ, with whom believers are one. This argument should make such sin unthinkable.

BELONGING TO GOD: Paul concludes by noting the Christian's body belongs to the Lord, is a member of Christ, and is the temple of the Holy Spirit.

18. OUTSIDE THE BODY: There is a sense in which sexual sin destroys a person like no other, because it is so intimate, entangling, and corrupting on the deepest human level. But here Paul is probably alluding to venereal disease, so prevalent and devastating in his day (and also today). No sin has greater potential to destroy the body.

19. NOT YOUR OWN: Because a believer's body belongs to the Lord, every act of fornication, adultery, or any other sin is committed in the sanctuary, the

Holy of Holies, where God dwells. In Old Testament times, the high priest only went into the Holy of Holies once a year, and then only after extensive cleansing, lest he be killed.

20. A PRICE: The precious blood of Christ.

GLORIFY GOD: The Christian's supreme purpose.

UNLEASHING THE TEXT

1) Why did Tamar ensnare Judah in sexual sin? Why did Judah commit that sin?

_____

_____

_____

_____

2) What did Judah reveal about his character when he ordered Tamar to be burned? What was he most concerned about in that situation?

_____

_____

_____

3) What was Judah admitting when he said that Tamar had been more righteous than he? What wasn't he admitting?

_____

_____

_____

_____

4) According to Paul, why is sexual sin such an affront to the Lord?

_____

_____

_____

Exploring the Meaning

Our sin can hinder God's blessings in our lives. Reuben was Jacob's firstborn son and would have naturally received the inheritance blessing. This would have placed on his shoulders the responsibility of leading his family and acting as the spiritual head—but his sin with his father's concubine effectively removed him from that position.

Reuben was not disinherited from Jacob's family, but he did lose some tremendous blessings that would have been his had he not committed this act against his father. In the same way, Christians do not lose their salvation when they sin, but they may very well deprive themselves of God's blessings in their lives.

God's greatest gift to His children is eternal life in His presence, but He goes far beyond that gift, working to pour out on us "every spiritual blessing in the heavenly places in Christ" (Ephesians 1:3). We hinder those blessings, however, when we stray from obedience to God's Word.

God can use even our failures to His glory. Our sin can hinder God's blessings in our lives, yet God continues to work within us—despite our failures—to make us more like His Son. Judah was no less guilty of sin than his brothers, yet the Lord would work faithfully to change his character and make him fit for service.

The Scriptures are filled with men and women who were imperfect and fell into sin—some of them grievous sins—while God continued to work in their lives. David, for example, committed adultery and murder, yet the Lord did not abandon him. David, like Judah, was in the genealogical line of Jesus.

The key to this is not in living a sinless life but in repenting of sin each time we fail. David demonstrated a heart for God when he acknowledged his sin and turned away from it, just as Judah ultimately would do. God will always accept a penitent heart, and He will turn our failures into His glory.

We are to flee from sexual immorality. It appears some of the Christians in Corinth, like Judah, were in the habit of visiting prostitutes. They had fallen prey to the faulty belief that because Jesus had given them freedom from their sins, they were free to go and commit more, or that sin could no longer touch them. Paul corrects them by saying they are to flee sexual sins, because those sins are committed with the human body, and that body is a temple of the Holy Spirit.

Jesus gave Himself as a ransom for our sins. He lived a perfect, sinless life in complete submission to the Father's will, yet He gave His life willingly on the cross to redeem us from our guilt: "The Son of Man did not come to be served, but to serve, and to give His life a ransom for many" (Matthew 20:28). By virtue of Jesus' resurrection and our union with Him, our bodies are members of Christ and belong to Him. We belong body, soul, and spirit only to the Lord, and any union outside of marriage is a betrayal of our union with Him.

REFLECTING ON THE TEXT

5) What do we learn of God's grace from the sordid affair of Judah and Tamar? How did the Lord bring glory to Himself through Judah's sin?

_____

_____

_____

6) What would have happened to Abraham's descendants if they had remained in Canaan? Why was it necessary for God to incubate them in Egypt?

_____

_____

_____

7) Consider the family of Jacob. How did sin produce bad consequences in their individual lives? How did Joseph present a stark contrast?

_____

_____

_____

8) What does Paul say about the freedom that believers have been given in Christ? How does that freedom relate to abstaining from immoral sexual relations?

_____

_____

_____

PERSONAL RESPONSE

9) When have you seen God's glory come out of someone's failures? How have you seen His grace at work in your own life?

_____

_____

_____

10) Is there sin in your life that is hindering God's full blessing? What changes in your heart might the Lord be asking you to make?

_____

_____

_____

4

JOSEPH THE SLAVE

Genesis 39:1–23

DRAWING NEAR

Why do we tend to draw closer to God during times of trial than times when everything is going well?

_____

_____

_____

THE CONTEXT

Let us now return to the story of Joseph, who had been sold into slavery by his brothers. A caravan of Midianites and Ishmaelites had brought him to Egypt when he was seventeen. We do not know what occurred along the way on that trip or what it was like to be bought and sold at a slave market in Egypt. But we can safely assume that none of it was pleasant.

Joseph was eventually purchased by a man named Potiphar, who held an important role in Pharaoh's kingdom as the captain of the guard. It is uncertain exactly what this role entailed, but it seems likely that it included oversight of Egypt's prisons. Potiphar was a wealthy and influential man, and it would have been profitable for a lowly slave like Joseph to find favor with him.

JOSEPH IN EGYPT

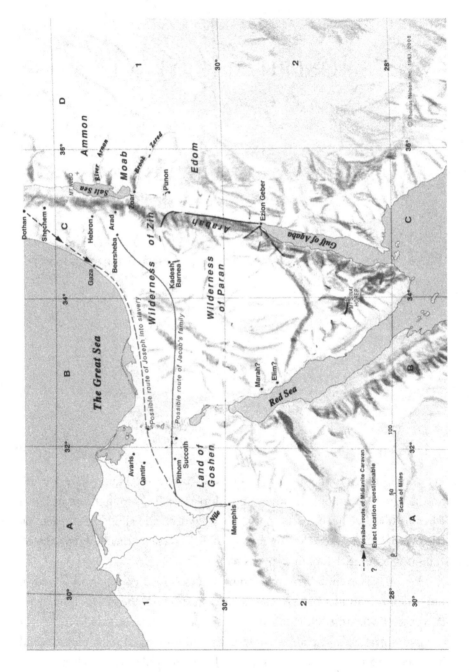

At this time Egypt was the most influential world power, and a place of great luxury and technology. The Egyptian culture and religious beliefs influenced all of Canaan and beyond, and its military was unsurpassed. By contrast, Jacob's family had been nomadic shepherds, roaming from place to place throughout Canaan for several generations. They lived in tents, while the Egyptians lived in permanent houses—and Egyptian architecture was grand even by modern standards.

Joseph was entering a nation that spoke a different language, operated under different cultural norms, and served foreign gods. To make matters worse, the Egyptians detested shepherds and considered such people unfit to even eat with. They bought and sold slaves, a social class that is at the bottom of any societal hierarchy. With his language and cultural differences, religious anomalies, social background, and lack of status as a slave, Joseph was about as low in Egyptian society as any human could sink. Add to this the fact that his own brothers had betrayed him, and we get a sense of the utter despair and heartbreak Joseph must have experienced.

Furthermore, as we read about Joseph's enslavement, we see how the "wheel of fortune" swung him violently from a position of favor at the top to a position of subjugation at the bottom . . . and then back up again . . . only to be dashed down once more. These dizzying swings of fortune would challenge anyone's faith, and most of us would respond with anger or despair. Yet Joseph's response was worlds apart. In fact, his reaction was not of this world at all but was instead focused on eternity.

KEYS TO THE TEXT

Read Genesis 39:1–23, noting the key words and phrases indicated below.

> SOLD INTO EGYPT: *The caravan takes Joseph to Egypt, where he is sold to a man named Potiphar, an officer of Pharaoh who serves as captain of the guard.*

39:1. TAKEN DOWN TO EGYPT: The map on page 38 shows the probable route that the caravan of Midianites and Ishmaelites followed. The distance was more than 200 miles, and the journey probably took a week or two to complete. Like Joseph, the Son of God would also one day be taken to Egypt:

"An angel of the Lord appeared to Joseph [the husband of Jesus' mother, Mary] in a dream, saying, 'Arise, take the young Child and His mother, flee to Egypt, and stay there until I bring you word'" (Matthew 2:13).

POTIPHAR: This name may have been a title for his position, just as *Pharaoh* was a title rather than a personal name.

OFFICER OF PHARAOH, CAPTAIN OF THE GUARD, AN EGYPTIAN: This lengthy description underscores the immense gulf that would have existed between Joseph and his new master. Potiphar was the captain of the guard, which meant he had a military background and was probably cultured and well educated—in contrast to Joseph's domestic upbringing. He was also a member of Pharaoh's retinue, quite possibly the chief of Pharaoh's personal bodyguard, which meant that he was probably of noble birth and royal connections. From a human perspective, there is little chance that such a man would pay any attention to a slave like Joseph.

2. THE LORD WAS WITH JOSEPH: It is easy for modern readers to gloss over this important fact, but if we put ourselves in Joseph's place, it is quite a startling statement. Joseph had gone out to the pastures to visit his brothers on his father's errand, not expecting anything unusual, and had ended up being taken to Egypt to live as a despised slave. It would be hard in those circumstances to believe that the Lord was with you, yet Joseph clung firmly to that conviction—and the Lord blessed him greatly.

HE WAS A SUCCESSFUL MAN: One way the Lord blessed Joseph was by bringing him success in all his endeavors. Potiphar evidently noticed that Joseph excelled in whatever tasks he was given, and that probably led to Joseph's quick advancement.

HE WAS IN THE HOUSE OF HIS MASTER: This indicates that Joseph had found favor with Potiphar and had been entrusted with household duties, as opposed to the more rigorous fieldwork. It also shows that Potiphar did not expect Joseph to run away and that he trusted him with access to his own home. Jewish tradition holds that Joseph was in Potiphar's household for a full year—a short time for one of his lowly stature to rise to a position of such trust.

3. HIS MASTER SAW THAT THE LORD WAS WITH HIM: This simple statement encapsulates the reason God chose the descendants of Abraham in the first place, as it was His plan to show forth His grace and character to all people. By observing the life of a faithful servant of God, the people of all nations could learn more about the character of God. Compare Joseph's description to Luke's

portrayal of Christ: "And the Child grew and became strong in spirit, filled with wisdom; and the grace of God was upon Him" (Luke 2:40).

4. OVERSEER OF HIS HOUSE: If Joseph's story had ended here, it would still have been a testament to the faithfulness of God toward those who follow Him. But the level of authority that Joseph had been given was not the end of God's plan. He had given Joseph prophetic dreams that still needed to be fulfilled (see Genesis 37:5–10).

6. HE LEFT ALL THAT HE HAD IN JOSEPH'S HAND: At this point Joseph may have felt things had turned out rather well, despite his previous sufferings. He might have become content to remain in that situation indefinitely. After all, it was (in worldly terms) an improvement over his nomadic shepherd's life. But this was not the Lord's plan, and his fortunes were about to change for the worse once again.

> POTIPHAR'S WIFE: *Joseph has risen to a position of honor that would be enough for any career—but his master's wife has some ideas of her own.*

JOSEPH WAS HANDSOME: He was eighteen or nineteen by this time and had grown into a handsome, strong, well-built young man. Those around him would have perceived him to be gifted, as he succeeded in everything to which he put his hand. Joseph was a man who turned heads.

7. LONGING EYES: The Hebrew for this phrase could be transliterated as "swept away by her eyes." Potiphar's wife was swept off her feet and carried away with her desire for this virile young man.

LIE WITH ME: Potiphar was probably busy with his duties, and the fact that he had no knowledge of his household affairs indicates that he may have been absent much of the time. Some scholars have even suggested that he may have been a eunuch, though the text makes no such mention of this. Whatever the circumstances, it would have been easy for Joseph to rationalize yielding to the demands of Potiphar's wife.

8. BUT HE REFUSED: Joseph was in the prime of his manhood and subject to the temptations of the flesh that are common to all people. He was also cut off from his family and loved ones, a stranger in a strange land, and quite likely felt great loneliness. Yet he demonstrated a steely determination to remain pure, even at the cost of denying strong fleshly desires.

9. How then can I do this great wickedness: Here was the foundation of Joseph's determination: he recognized that he was directly accountable to God for his actions. He recognized that all sin is ultimately committed against God Himself, and this perspective helped him remain strong. Jesus also faced temptation at the hands of Satan, and He too stood firm against it. Like Joseph, He understood that all sin is ultimately against God. He resisted the devil's wiles by focusing on the Word of God.

10. she spoke to Joseph day by day: It is difficult enough to resist powerful temptation once, but having it repeated day after day can seem intolerable. Yet God does not ever permit us to be tempted beyond the point of endurance: "No temptation has overtaken you except such as is common to man; but God is faithful, who will not allow you to be tempted beyond what you are able, but with the temptation will also make the way of escape, that you may be able to bear it" (1 Corinthians 10:13).

he did not heed her: Joseph went beyond the point of repeatedly refusing her advances; he refused even to discuss it with her. Such a debate would only have increased his tempter's opportunities. It always does.

or to be with her: In addition to refusing to discuss the issue, Joseph refused to even be in her company. If we follow Joseph's example, we will avoid the very company of those who suggest we disregard God's Word.

Falsely Accused: Potiphar's wife is forced to recognize that Joseph will not yield to her sinful demands—and she responds with venom.

11. Joseph went into the house to do his work: In the midst of this terrific persecution, Joseph remained faithful to his duties. This is another aspect of his faithfulness to God: he steadfastly refused to sin while also steadfastly remaining faithful to what God had given him to do. It is important to realize, however, that even our complete faithfulness will not protect us from facing temptation. The Lord does permit temptation to enter our lives for the purpose of making us more like Christ.

12. he left his garment in her hand, and fled and ran outside: Jesus said, "If your eye causes you to sin, pluck it out. It is better for you to enter the kingdom of God with one eye, rather than having two eyes, to be cast into hell fire" (Mark 9:47). Paul wrote, "Flee also youthful lusts" (2 Timothy

2:22). Thousands of years in advance of these admonitions from Paul and Christ, Joseph was already responding in Christlike fashion to this persistent woman's advances.

13. WHEN SHE SAW THAT HE HAD LEFT HIS GARMENT IN HER HAND: Even Potiphar's wife eventually was forced to recognize that Joseph was not going to yield to her temptations. In our lives there will be times when our faithfulness will cause the world to hate us, just as was the case with Joseph.

14. TO MOCK US: Those who are committed to the world's system will resent the people of God. When we speak out against the world's wickedness, we will face the hatred of many, and their responses will be to accuse us of being judgmental and self-righteous. Even Lot found this to be true when he urged the men of Sodom not to attack the Lord's angels: "Then they said, 'This one came in to stay here, and he keeps acting as a judge; now we will deal worse with you than with them.' So they pressed hard against the man Lot, and came near to break down the door" (Genesis 19:9). The Jews would later use this same false accusation against Jesus, suggesting to their Roman rulers that He was leading a rebellion against Rome (see John 19:12).

16. SHE KEPT HIS GARMENT WITH HER: From a human perspective, Joseph did not stand a chance against this false accusation. He had risen to authority in Potiphar's home, yet he was still a slave—and a Hebrew slave, at that. It was his word against the word of his master's wife, and the outcome seemed clear from the beginning. Yet this does not account for the sovereignty of God. The outcome of the situation was entirely in the Lord's hands, no matter what the odds were against Joseph.

OFF TO PRISON: *Joseph is now brought to a prison cell, which God will use as a training ground to help him learn the skills he will need for the next phase of his life.*

19. HIS MASTER HEARD THE WORDS: When Potiphar heard his wife's false accusations that Joseph had attempted to rape her, his anger was aroused. Such anger would have been justified if he truly believed what his wife had told him. Nevertheless, neither he nor his wife could frustrate the Lord's plans for Joseph's life. In fact, Potiphar inadvertently furthered God's plans.

20. PUT HIM INTO THE PRISON: It is quite possible that Potiphar was in charge over this prison, though he probably was not the warden. From a human

perspective, this must have seemed a dead end for Joseph. He was a mere slave, the lowest class of humanity in a foreign land, with no friends or family to assist him. But the Lord wanted him in that specific prison at that specific time because He had a specific task for Joseph to perform there. Even when circumstances seem completely hopeless and out of control, God is completely *in* control. We have the glorious hope of His faithfulness.

A PLACE WHERE THE KING'S PRISONERS WERE CONFINED: If Joseph had been sent to a different prison, he would never have met Pharaoh's chief butler. When we trust God's sovereignty, He uses us for His purposes wherever we are.

21. BUT THE LORD WAS WITH JOSEPH: Once again, it would have been all too easy for Joseph to fall into despair, believing the Lord had abandoned him or had been unfaithful. Yet Joseph clung to his conviction that the Lord is faithful and will never abandon His children. His example shows us that even in the midst of seemingly hopeless circumstances, the Lord shows us His mercy and faithfulness. When we focus on His sovereignty in our lives, we will see that He is working all things together for His glory—even in the darkest hours.

22. COMMITTED TO JOSEPH'S HAND ALL THE PRISONERS: This would prove to be important in Joseph's future. It was another proof that God was in complete control over all Joseph's circumstances.

23. WHATEVER HE DID, THE LORD MADE IT PROSPER: Joseph did not find favor in the eyes of the warden simply because he was a diligent worker but also because the Lord caused it to happen. Once again, God was blessing Joseph's faithfulness, and that blessing was becoming evident to the people around him. Wherever he went, whether slave or free, Joseph was a blessing to those around him. This is what it means to be one of God's children.

UNLEASHING THE TEXT

1) Put yourself in Joseph's place. How would you have reacted if you had found yourself in a slave caravan heading toward Egypt? How would you have responded to your new masters?

_____

_____

_____

2) What evidence is there that God was in control of Joseph's circumstances? How much of God's control would Joseph have seen at the time?

_____

_____

_____

3) In what ways was Joseph faithful to the Lord during his time in Potiphar's house?

_____

_____

_____

4) Why did Joseph rise so quickly to a position of authority? What part did God play in those events? What part did Joseph play?

_____

_____

_____

EXPLORING THE MEANING

God is in control of every event in our lives—both good and bad. It is startling to consider the dramatic rises and falls in Joseph's fortunes—and the story isn't even finished yet. We have the ability to read his history and readily see the hand of God at work in his life, but it was not so easy for Joseph when he was living through these events. It would have been much easier for him to yield to despair or bitterness.

But God had absolute control over all these events, and He was not haphazard in the things He allowed Joseph to endure. During his tenure in Potiphar's household, for example, Joseph learned important managerial skills that he would need later in life. God saw far beyond the immediate horizon of his day-to-day existence, and His plan was perfect. He knows exactly what each of His children needs to learn and what qualities he or she must develop in fulfilling that plan.

When we undergo deep suffering or elevated success, it is easy to lose sight of this important principle. The Lord is in control of everything that touches us—including the mundane, daily grind of ordinary life, which itself can be the most valuable training in the long run. We make the most of His character development when we keep this truth in mind.

Do not try to simply endure strong temptation—run away! There is much that goes unstated in this portion of Joseph's story. For instance, the Bible does not tell us what powerful emotions he was experiencing as a slave in Egypt. Joseph was a healthy young man in his prime, cut off from family and friends, and living in a foreign land. The temptations of Potiphar's wife must have been powerful indeed.

Yet Joseph demonstrated the correct way to deal with such temptations: he fled! He refused to discuss the subject with the one who tempted him and declined even to be in her company. He evidently made a point of trying never to be alone in the house with her, and on the last occasion did so only inadvertently. When he found himself in that dangerous predicament, he quite literally ran away, even to the point of leaving his cloak in her hands.

Some situations will require you to persevere in daily decisions to please your heavenly Father, while others will only be overcome by running away. But whatever your situation, the Bible tells you to "be sober, be vigilant; because your adversary the devil walks about like a roaring lion, seeking whom he may devour." You are to "resist him, steadfast in the faith, knowing that the same sufferings are experienced by your brotherhood in the world" (1 Peter 5:8–9). Sometimes, the best way to resist a roaring lion is to flee.

The Lord blesses us when we are obedient. It almost seems incongruous to read that the Lord was blessing Joseph by sending him into Egypt as a slave, but

God's purposes go far beyond the immediate moment. The Lord had placed Joseph in a situation over which he had no control, but there was one thing that he *could* control: his responses to that situation.

Joseph focused on doing the things that he was given to do—which meant obeying his slave master and doing his work carefully and earnestly. There are times when our greatest act of obedience to the Lord is simply to submit humbly to the circumstances that are beyond our control. Our submission to His will allows our Father to pour out His fullest blessings into our lives. "Whatever your hand finds to do, do it with your might" (Ecclesiastes 9:10). In the long run, our Father will bless that attitude.

REFLECTING ON THE TEXT

5) What excuses might Joseph have made for giving in to the advances from Potiphar's wife?

_____

_____

_____

6) How did Joseph overcome the temptations of Potiphar's wife? What was his focus during that struggle?

_____

_____

7) What aspects of Joseph's situation were beyond his power to change? What aspects were within his control?

_____

_____

_____

8) When have you seen the Lord bring great blessing out of sorrow in your own life or the life of someone you know?

_____

_____

_____

_____

PERSONAL RESPONSE

9) What situations in your life are beyond your power to change? How would the Lord have you respond to those situations?

_____

_____

_____

_____

10) What people might be watching your life to see whether Christianity is true? Is your life providing a faithful witness to the truth of the gospel?

_____

_____

_____

_____

_____

5

PHARAOH'S CHIEF BUTLER
Genesis 40:1–23

DRAWING NEAR

When is a time in your life that someone forgot something important to you?
How did you feel? How did you react?

_____

_____

_____

THE CONTEXT

In the last study, we saw how Potiphar's wife falsely accused Joseph because he
would not give in to her advances, and as a result Joseph was thrown into prison.
He remained there for many years, and certainly it would have seemed that
there was little hope of his ever being exonerated and set free. But Joseph never
lost heart, because he knew the Lord was in control of all his circumstances. He
trusted that God would fulfill the prophecies of his youthful dreams.

Meanwhile, as Joseph worked diligently in the prison, two men of high
rank in Pharaoh's court had some problems of their own. We are not told
what provoked the king's anger toward them, but something serious occurred.
The chief butler and chief baker were personally responsible for everything

49

Pharaoh ate and drank. This included the weighty responsibility of ensuring nobody tried to poison the king. It is quite possible such an attempt was made, or some political intrigue was uncovered at court, because the king evidently held one of these two men responsible.

It might have taken some time for Pharaoh to sort out who was responsible and who was guilty, for the chief butler and chief baker sat in prison for about a year. By the time they were released, however, the king had arrived at a conclusion: one of them was innocent and should be set free, while the other must die. Joseph knew nothing of these intrigues, of course, yet he would become an important player in the drama.

Fortunately for all concerned, God was still in control.

KEYS TO THE TEXT

Read Genesis 40:1–23, noting the key words and phrases indicated below.

> THE RIGHT PLACE AT THE RIGHT TIME: *The Lord has Joseph spend time in prison so he can meet the chief butler. The Lord works out the details in his life—and in the lives of others—for His greater purpose.*

40:1. AFTER THESE THINGS: Joseph had probably been in prison a fair amount of time when these events occurred, as the prison warden had already come to trust him implicitly.

THE BUTLER AND THE BAKER: Despite their humble-sounding titles, these were men of high authority and responsibility. Both men had access to what Pharaoh ate and drank, so they had to be completely trustworthy and beyond the influence of the king's enemies. It was part of God's plan that these two men should wind up in prison at this time because He was at work in *their* lives as well as in Joseph's life. The Lord was working out a plan for Joseph and for Jacob's entire family, but He was also working out His plans for these two men. God is absolutely sovereign in all affairs.

THE KING OF EGYPT: He should be identified as Senusert II, who reigned in Egypt from 1894–1878 BC.

2. PHARAOH WAS ANGRY: We are not told what these two men had done, or even whether they were guilty of a crime. However, the end result for the chief

baker would suggest that the king suspected them of disloyalty. Because each of the men had the potential of poisoning him, Pharaoh could not take chances.

3. CAPTAIN OF THE GUARD: This may well have been Potiphar, who was called the captain of the guard (see Genesis 39:1). If so, it is likely that he placed Joseph in charge of these two important prisoners because he had proven himself trustworthy in the past.

THE PLACE WHERE JOSEPH WAS CONFINED: Had Potiphar's wife not falsely accused Joseph, he would not have been in the prison at this time. If the chief butler and chief baker had not angered Pharaoh, *they* would not have been in prison at this time. Indeed, if Joseph's brothers had not sold him into slavery, he would not have been in Egypt at all. In all these events, we see the will of God working through circumstances and men's actions—even wicked actions—to bring about His plan.

> JOSEPH THE SERVANT: *In spite of his seemingly hopeless situation, Joseph maintains his servant spirit and never loses his focus on following God's will.*

4. HE SERVED THEM: Service was a hallmark of Joseph's life, and he made it a practice to put the concerns of others before his own. As we will see in the next study, this was the very characteristic that would one day place him in a position to be elevated to Pharaoh's right hand.

THEY WERE IN CUSTODY FOR A WHILE: Again, this indicates Joseph was probably in prison for many years.

5. HAD A DREAM: As Joseph sat in prison and interpreted the dreams of other men, he must have been bitterly reminded of his own prophetic dream and how it predicted a position of authority for himself. It is truly remarkable that this young man never gave way to hopelessness but always waited for God to prove Himself faithful. The Lord used Joseph's dreams to provide him with encouragement and hope during times of despair, but He also used them to prepare him for the future. In the same way, God often sends experiences into our lives that prepare us for some upcoming task—though we may have no idea at the time what we are being prepared for.

WITH ITS OWN INTERPRETATION: Oneiromancy, the practice of interpreting dreams, flourished in ancient Egypt because dreams were thought to determine the future. Both Egypt and Babylon developed a professional class of dream interpreters (see Daniel 2:2), and some 500 years later a detailed manual of dream interpretation would be compiled. Later, in Deuteronomy 13:1–5, Moses told the Israelites that such dream interpreters were part of ancient false religion and should be avoided.

6. JOSEPH CAME IN TO THEM IN THE MORNING: He probably waited on these important men daily, serving them as their own private butler. It must have seemed ironic to the chief butler, many years later, when he saw the roles were reversed.

SAW THAT THEY WERE SAD: Here we see Joseph's servant spirit in action. If anyone had reason to be sad it was Joseph, who was in prison because of a false accusation by a powerful woman—and indeed, because of a terrible betrayal by his own brothers. But Joseph was not consumed by his woes. Instead, he was quick to show compassion for another person's suffering, even if that suffering was nothing compared to his own.

7. WHY DO YOU LOOK SO SAD TODAY? A more common response might have been, "You think *you* have problems?" But Joseph was genuinely concerned to serve these men and to do anything in his power to remove their sorrow.

> DREAM INTERPRETATIONS: *In addition to maintaining his servant attitude, Joseph retains his God-given ability to interpret dreams. This will prove important as he steps into the next chapter of God's plan for his life.*

THERE IS NO INTERPRETER OF IT: Unlike Joseph, neither the chief butler nor the chief baker understood the significance of their dreams.

8. DO NOT INTERPRETATIONS BELONG TO GOD? Joseph was careful to recognize God as the source of all understanding for dreams and give Him the credit for it. Daniel, the only other Hebrew in the Bible whom God allowed to accurately interpret revelatory dreams, was just as careful to do so (see Daniel 2:28). Significantly, God chose both men to play an important role for Israel while serving pagan monarchs.

9. A VINE WAS BEFORE ME: Consistent with his duty as the cupbearer to the king, the chief butler dreamed of a drink prepared for Pharaoh.

13. PHARAOH WILL LIFT UP YOUR HEAD: There is an ironic wordplay at work in Joseph's statement. The phrase "lift up your head" in the original Hebrew could mean that Pharaoh was about to bestow great honor on the

man—as was true in this case. However, it could also mean that Pharaoh was about to *literally* lift up the man's head by removing it from his body. This, in fact, was what happened with the chief baker.

14. REMEMBER ME WHEN IT IS WELL WITH YOU: Joseph knew that butlers had the ear of kings. So he appealed to this man, whose future was now secure, to speak a word on his behalf for his freedom. This is the only record we have of Joseph looking after his own interests, and it shows both restraint and wisdom on his part. He had not asked for anything in return for his service to the chief butler, always placing the interests of others above his own. But he also took advantage of a legitimate opportunity to request help in undoing the injustice.

> CHARACTER STUDY: *The dreams the two men have give us insights into their characters. One is a faithful servant, while the other is just self-serving.*

16. THE CHIEF BAKER SAW THAT THE INTERPRETATION WAS GOOD: The chief baker was evidently not interested in having Joseph interpret his dream unless he could be confident the interpretation would be good. He seems to have been more concerned with personal gain than with learning the truth.

I ALSO WAS IN MY DREAM: Here is another subtle insight into this man's nature. He saw himself as the center point of his dream—"I was in my dream"—whereas the chief butler saw the vine as the centerpiece (see verse 9).

17. THE BIRDS ATE THEM: Notice that in the chief baker's dream, he was careless of his responsibility before Pharaoh, allowing the birds to eat the bread right off his head. The chief butler's dream, by contrast, showed him thinking of his master at all times, finding a succulent vine and making wine for Pharaoh. The dreams suggest that the chief butler was a faithful servant, while the chief baker was not.

19. PHARAOH WILL LIFT OFF YOUR HEAD: The phrase Joseph used in the interpretation for the baker's dream is identical to the one he used for the butler, but with one notable addition: the words "from you." Pharaoh was going to "lift up" the butler to a place of authority, but "lift off" the baker's head.

20. PHARAOH'S BIRTHDAY: The Rosetta Stone, discovered in AD 1799, records a custom of pharaohs releasing prisoners on their birthday. However, at this party held for his servants, Pharaoh rendered two very different kinds of judgment.

21. HE HANGED THE CHIEF BAKER: Apparently the chief baker was be-headed, and then his corpse was either hung from a tree branch or gallows or impaled. It was a sign of utter disgrace. The fate of these two men presents us with the flip side of God's sovereignty: the free will of mankind. The chief baker apparently *had* committed some crime against Pharaoh, and he ended up being executed. The Lord permits men and women to make their own choices—even when those choices lead to bad consequences.

23. THE CHIEF BUTLER DID NOT REMEMBER JOSEPH: Here we are given another insight into the chief butler's character. In spite of the service Joseph had performed, he did not remember Joseph's request. This suggests that the chief butler's faithfulness was limited: he was a faithful servant to Pharaoh but disregarded those beneath his social caste. Joseph, on the other hand, was faithful to any task the Lord placed before him, and he served both the high and the low equally.

BUT FORGOT HIM: This must have been a crushing blow to Joseph. He was likely filled with hope when he made such an important friend as the chief butler, and he might have thought he could see how the Lord was going to work things together to free him from prison. The long process of realizing he had, in fact, been forgotten must have been painful for him. What's worse, he probably remained in prison for a couple of years after the chief butler left, and it must have seemed as if he would spend the rest of his life there. Perhaps he even won-dered whether he had misinterpreted his prophetic dreams years before. But God had given him a promise, and the Lord always keeps His promises.

Unleashing the Text

1) If you had been in Joseph's place, how would you have felt as a slave in prison? How would you have reacted to the butler and baker's sadness?

_____

_____

_____

_____

2) If you had been in the butler's place, how would you have responded to Joseph's interpretation of your dream? How would you have responded if you were in the baker's place?

_____

_____

_____

3) What can we infer about the character of the butler and the baker based on their respective dreams? What can we infer about their motives?

_____

_____

_____

4) Why do you think the butler forgot Joseph? How might he have felt when he saw Joseph raised to Pharaoh's right hand?

_____

_____

_____

EXPLORING THE MEANING

God's people should be ready and willing to serve in all situations. Joseph had been treated treacherously by many people, including his own brothers, in situations where he was innocent of any wrongdoing. He had languished in prison for several years under a false accusation and had little hope of ever being released. It would be understandable if he had sulked and looked after his own interests.

But again, we find that is not how Joseph responded. When he discovered an opportunity to serve others, he did so willingly and cheerfully. The concerns of the chief butler were puny compared to Joseph's, yet Joseph did not chide him for sulking over a strange dream. Instead, he listened to the dream, gave God credit for the interpretation, and explained to the butler what was about to happen.

Jesus Christ is another example of one who never missed an opportunity to serve others—even though He was the Creator of the universe. He humbled Himself before His disciples when He washed their feet, and He submitted Himself to a horrible death on the cross. As Paul would later write, Christ Jesus "made Himself of no reputation, taking the form of a bondservant, and coming in the likeness of men . . . He humbled Himself and became obedient to the point of death" (Philippians 2:7–8). Christians are called to follow Jesus' example and serve one another cheerfully and freely.

Remember those who have helped you in the past. The chief butler had a tremendously important position in Pharaoh's court, and he was probably responsible for a full staff of assistants—to say nothing of the health and welfare of the king. The cares and duties of his career probably crowded Joseph out of his mind. Nevertheless, he had a responsibility to demonstrate his gratitude for Joseph's service to him, and few people were in a better position to help Joseph than he.

There are undoubtedly many people who have been influential for good in your life. Perhaps this was the person who led you to salvation, or the Sunday school teachers who trained you, or a friend who was always available when you needed someone to talk with. The list will get long if you ask the Lord to bring to mind the people who have helped you in the past.

You can show your gratitude to such people by praying for them, by returning favors when they need help, or even just spending time with them when they are feeling lonely. Ask the Lord to remind you of such people in your life and show how you can return His love to them.

Whatever the Lord gives you to do, do it with all your might. Joseph demonstrated this principle by carrying out every task the Lord gave to him with vigor and diligence. When he was in Potiphar's household, he served his master with such distinction that he was elevated to a place of authority. When a false accusation landed him in prison, he served the warden with such distinction that he was again given a leadership role. Later, as we will see in the next study, he served with distinction as second in command to the king.

In each of these positions Joseph carried out his work with all his might, which serves as an excellent example of what the Lord calls His people to do. Whatever job He gives us, we are to do it with the attitude that we are serving God directly rather than men. The Scriptures confirm this counsel: "Whatever your hand finds to do, do it with your might; for there is no work or device or knowledge or wisdom in the grave where you are going" (Ecclesiastes 9:10). "And whatever you do, do it heartily, as to the Lord and not to men, knowing that from the Lord you will receive the reward of the inheritance; for you serve the Lord Christ" (Colossians 3:23–24).

REFLECTING ON THE TEXT

5) What motivated Joseph to serve the butler and baker without grumbling?

_____

_____

_____

6) Why did the captain of the guard give Joseph responsibility for the chief butler and chief baker? What does this reveal about Joseph's character?

_____

_____

_____

_____

7) Why did Joseph say the interpretation of dreams belongs to God? What does this reveal about his faith?

_____

_____

_____

8) What does it mean to do something "as to the Lord and not to men"? What difference can such an attitude make in your performance at work? At home? At church?

_____

_____

PERSONAL RESPONSE

9) Make a list below of people who have helped you in the past, and then ask the Lord to show you how you can be of help to them in the future.

_____

_____

_____

10) What jobs has the Lord given you to do in the coming week? How can you fulfill those responsibilities "as to the Lord and not to men"?

_____

_____

_____

_____

6

JOSEPH THE RULER
Genesis 41:1–57

DRAWING NEAR

In what positions of leadership has God placed you? What training in the "school of life" did you go through to learn your leadership skills?

_____

_____

_____

THE CONTEXT

As we previously discussed, Joseph met Pharaoh's chief butler—an important member of the king's household—when the two were in prison together. When Joseph accurately interpreted the man's dream, he asked the butler to speak on his behalf and help secure his release. But the butler forgot about Joseph . . . until one day when Pharaoh had a troubling dream himself. When none of the king's wise men could interpret it, the butler suddenly remembered Joseph's unique gifts.

Pharaoh immediately sent for Joseph to come out of the prison, and, as we will see in this study, the Lord gave Joseph the correct interpretation of the dream. In this way God told Pharaoh that there would be seven years of plenty in the land, with undreamed-of harvests and abundance, but that this time would be followed by seven years of drought. The drought would be so severe that it would eat up all the excess of the previous years of plenty and threaten all peoples in the known world.

Of course, God would not be caught off guard by this development. He had been planning for this contingency all along and had trained up a special man to lead the world through it. This man was none other than Joseph, and the training he received would enable him to lead Egypt through a set of circumstances that have produced rebellion and even revolution in other nations at other times. In the passages we will study today, we will discover how the years Joseph spent as a slave in Potiphar's house and in prison actually prepared him to do this most difficult job.

KEYS TO THE TEXT

Read Genesis 41:1–57, noting the key words and phrases indicated below.

> THE BUTLER REMEMBERS: *Joseph languishes in prison for another two years, waiting for the chief butler to help him. It takes a crisis at court to jog his memory.*

41:1. AT THE END OF TWO FULL YEARS: Once again, from a human perspective there was no hope that Joseph would ever get out of prison alive. But God was about to prove Himself faithful to His servant.

THE RIVER: Probably the Nile River, which dominated Egyptian life.

8. THE MAGICIANS OF EGYPT: These were likely astrologers and practitioners of other pagan mysteries. Moses would later confront them when the time came for Israel to leave Egypt (see Exodus 7:11–13). In both instances, the Lord's power was proven to be the only source of truth.

NO ONE WHO COULD INTERPRET: The combined expertise of a full council of Pharaoh's advisers and dream experts, all of whom had been summoned into his presence, failed to provide an interpretation of the two disturbing dreams. Without knowing it, they had just set the stage for Joseph's entrance on the scene.

9. I REMEMBER MY FAULTS THIS DAY: With his memory suitably prompted, the butler apologized for his neglect and informed Pharaoh of the Hebrew prisoner named Joseph who had accurately interpreted his dream two

years before. In this the chief butler may have been an opportunist, conveniently remembering Joseph only when it was profitable to himself, yet his confession of fault does seem sincere.

> PHARAOH'S DREAM: *Because none of Pharaoh's own wise men can interpret the dream, he follows the chief butler's advice and calls upon Joseph.*

14. PHARAOH SENT AND CALLED JOSEPH: The urgent summons had Joseph in front of Pharaoh with minimum delay, in prized, clean-shaven Egyptian style for a proper appearance. Joseph's faithful service had at last received its reward: he was suddenly released from prison.

16. IT IS NOT IN ME: Just as Joseph had done when he interpreted the dreams of the chief butler and chief baker, he deprecated any innate ability of his own. Joseph advised at the outset that the answer Pharaoh desired could only come from God.

28. GOD HAS SHOWN PHARAOH WHAT HE IS ABOUT TO DO: With precision, Joseph told Pharaoh the meaning of his dream: there would be seven years of plenty, followed by seven years of devastating famine. Joseph's interpretation kept the focus fixed on what God had determined for Egypt.

33. LET PHARAOH SELECT A DISCERNING AND WISE MAN: Incongruously, Joseph, a slave and a prisoner, appended to the dream interpretation a long-term strategy for establishing reserves to meet the future need. He also included advice on the quality of the man whom Pharaoh should choose to oversee preparations and head up the project. Famines had ravaged Egypt before, but this time divine warning permitted serious and sustained advance planning.

34. COLLECT ONE-FIFTH OF THE PRODUCE OF THE LAND OF EGYPT: The man whom Pharaoh chose to oversee the project was to take advantage of the coming seven years of plenty by taxing the nation at twenty percent of all crops. He was to set up storage centers around Egypt and hold that food in reserve for the seven years of famine to follow.

> JOSEPH IS ELEVATED: *Pharaoh recognizes that God is with Joseph and immediately places him in command over all Egypt.*

38. A MAN IN WHOM IS THE SPIRIT OF GOD: Once again we see that God's involvement in the life of Joseph was readily apparent to those around

him. Joseph had made himself available to God, accepting the circumstances the Lord brought into his life, and as a result even Pharaoh could discern that the Spirit of the Lord was working in him.

39. GOD HAS SHOWN YOU ALL THIS: What an amazing statement, spoken to a slave! Yet Joseph did not allow himself to become puffed up by the great things God had done through him.

40. YOU SHALL BE OVER MY HOUSE: This was precisely the same arrangement Joseph had in Potiphar's household—but on a much grander scale. He became the head over all Egypt, the greatest nation on earth in his day, and ruled with absolute authority, subject only to Pharaoh himself. Yet again, we must remember the Lord had prepared him for this powerful position through the experiences he had endured as a slave in Potiphar's house. Had Joseph not submitted to the Lord's training as a slave, he would not have been equipped for this tremendous responsibility.

41. I HAVE SET YOU OVER ALL THE LAND OF EGYPT: Joseph was elevated to the right hand of Pharaoh, giving him the authority to speak on Pharaoh's behalf. The New Testament shows us that Jesus is seated at the right hand of God: "Therefore being exalted to the right hand of God, and having received from the Father the promise of the Holy Spirit, He poured out this which you now see and hear. For David did not ascend into the heavens, but he says himself: 'The LORD said to my Lord, "Sit at my right hand, till I make your enemies your footstool."' Therefore let all the house of Israel know assuredly that God has made this Jesus, whom you crucified, both Lord and Christ" (Acts 2:33–36). "But to which of the angels has He ever said: 'Sit at my right hand, till I make your enemies your footstool'?" (Hebrews 1:13).

42. SIGNET RING: This was an emblem of office that gave Joseph authority to make laws and proclamations throughout Egypt. Similarly, Jesus would be given the authority of His Father: "He who has seen Me has seen the Father; so how can you say, 'Show us the Father'? Do you not believe that I am in the Father, and the Father in Me? The words that I speak to you I do not speak on My own authority; but the Father who dwells in Me does the works" (John 14:9–10).

GARMENTS OF FINE LINEN . . . GOLD CHAIN: The fine linen and gold chain indicated Joseph's status as a high-ranking member of Pharaoh's own household. There is a wonderful example in this passage of God's faithfulness. As you will recall from study 2, Joseph had been given a special robe by his father, which indicated that Jacob held him in high esteem among his brothers.

His brothers had stripped him of that robe and sold him into slavery, but now, after many years of faithfulness, Joseph had his robe returned—with interest. His new clothing represented an even higher degree of honor and esteem than what he had lost previously.

43. AND HE HAD HIM RIDE IN THE SECOND CHARIOT: Pharaoh bestowed other awards appropriate to Joseph's promotion, including official and recognizable transportation. This "second chariot" indicated that Joseph was second-in-command.

BOW THE KNEE! All Egypt was compelled to bow before Joseph.

44. WITHOUT YOUR CONSENT NO MAN MAY LIFT HIS HAND OR FOOT: There is a wonderful divine justice in this decree. Joseph had humbly submitted himself to the violence of his brothers when they lifted their hands against him, and he had continued to submit himself under the hand of God's training. As a result, he was found fit to judge over the "lifting of hands" throughout the nation of Egypt.

45. PHARAOH CALLED JOSEPH'S NAME ZAPHNATH-PAANEAH: The meaning of this name is unclear, but it might mean "God speaks and He lives." It was common in the ancient world to give a person a new name when he became the subject of a foreign king. In the same way, the Lord will give each of His children new names in His eternal kingdom (see Revelation 2:17), and Jesus Himself will bear a new name for all eternity: King of Kings and Lord of Lords (see Revelation 19:16).

JOSEPH'S BLESSINGS: The Lord now restores to Joseph far more than what he had lost when sold into slavery.

46. JOSEPH WAS THIRTY YEARS OLD: He was seventeen when he was sold into slavery, so he had endured thirteen years of captivity and enslavement.

49. UNTIL HE STOPPED COUNTING, FOR IT WAS IMMEASURABLE: This is how the Lord blesses those who obey Him, pouring out blessings in immeasurable abundance. "'Try Me now in this,' says the LORD of hosts, 'if I will not open for you the windows of heaven and pour out for you such blessing that there will not be room enough to receive it'" (Malachi 3:10).

ON: One of the four great Egyptian cities, also called Heliopolis, which was known as the chief city of the sun god, Ra. It was located approximately nineteen miles north of ancient Memphis.

51. MANASSEH: meaning "causing to forget." The Lord blessed Joseph so abundantly that it was as if he had never suffered in the first place. Even his lost family had been restored to the extent that he forgot his grief.

52. EPHRAIM: meaning "double fruit." Like Joseph, Job had also suffered tremendously, but the Lord rewarded his faithfulness with double what he had lost (see Job 42:10). Now he was rewarding Joseph the same way.

55. GO TO JOSEPH: Joseph's authority remained intact, and after seven years Pharaoh still fully trusted his vizier. Joseph dispensed the food supplies by sale to Egyptians and others.

57. ALL COUNTRIES CAME TO JOSEPH: The use of hyperbole with the word *all* emphatically indicates the widespread ravaging impact of famine far beyond Egypt's borders. She had indeed become the "breadbasket" of the ancient world.

THE FAMINE WAS SEVERE IN ALL LANDS: Pharaoh's dream, prophesying a fourteen-year cycle of plenty and famine, was fulfilled completely.

UNLEASHING THE TEXT

1) How do you think Joseph felt when he was whisked out of prison and made the ruler of all Egypt? How would you have reacted in that situation?

_____

_____

_____

2) If you were in Joseph's place, what temptations might you have faced concerning those who had mistreated you in the past? How did Joseph treat those people?

_____

_____

_____

3) How had God prepared Joseph to take command in Egypt? Give specific examples.

_____

_____

_____

4) If you had been an Egyptian landowner, how might you have reacted to Joseph's acts as your sovereign? How do you react to civic obligations in your own life?

_____

_____

_____

EXPLORING THE MEANING

A godly leader is first a godly follower. Joseph demonstrated this principle in his own life. God tested him when he was sold into slavery in Egypt, and Joseph remained faithful. The Lord gave him lowly jobs as a slave to Potiphar, and later as a falsely accused prisoner, and Joseph performed those jobs faithfully.

As we have seen, these roles as slave and prisoner were actually preparing Joseph for his role as a powerful leader—but he did not know it at the time. His focus was merely on obeying God and diligently performing whatever tasks he had been given to do. He had learned the lesson of obeying authority, whether that authority was a slave master or a prison guard.

The reason why submission is such an important trait in a leader is because godly leaders will *continue to be in submission* regardless of their position of authority. Godly leaders will always be in submission to the Word of God, and for this reason they must learn to submit to the will of God. Joseph demonstrated he understood this principle throughout his life. He submitted to his masters in Egypt, believed the prophecy the Lord had given through Pharaoh's dreams, and then acted accordingly.

The Lord appoints our leaders, even in the realm of worldly politics. This principle can seem hard for us to accept at times, especially when a nation's leaders are ungodly and unjust. This was certainly the case in Israel and Judah under numerous wicked kings: Elijah suffered under the ungodly leadership of King Ahab and his notorious wife, Jezebel; Jeremiah suffered under the leadership of King Jehoiakim; and Jesus Himself submitted to the unwise authority of the Romans when He was sent to the cross.

God's people are called to submit themselves to those in authority—in the home, at church, in the workplace, and in society as a whole. As Paul wrote, "Let every soul be subject to the governing authorities. For there is no authority except from God, and the authorities that exist are appointed by God. Therefore whoever resists the authority resists the ordinance of God, and those who resist will bring judgment on themselves" (Romans 13:1–2).

There may be times when the authority figures over us seem inept or unjust or even openly wicked. Yet we must recognize their authority comes from God, and He has placed us under it for His purposes. There can be few situations more unjust than slavery, yet Joseph submitted—and God blessed his faithfulness.

The Lord uses trials to prepare us for greater tasks. Joseph suffered greatly when his brothers betrayed him and when Potiphar's wife falsely accused him. But God permitted these trials, even though it might have been hard for Joseph to see His hand at the time. The Lord was using these trials to strengthen Joseph's faith and teach him practical lessons he would need later. Joseph had no idea that he would eventually rule over all Egypt, and he consequently could not have prepared himself with the skills that would be required. Only the Lord knew those things, and He used disappointments, setbacks, slavery, and imprisonment to train Joseph for the future.

We may not become world leaders, but the Lord's plans for our future are still important in the eternal scheme. And the day will come when all of His people shall rule the world—in fact, we will rule with Him over all creation, for all eternity. He is preparing each of us now to be ready for that great role of leadership, and He uses every circumstance in our lives for our spiritual good—including suffering and hardship. "And we know that all things work together for good to those who love God, to those who are the called according to His purpose" (Romans 8:28).

REFLECTING ON THE TEXT

5) Why did God send such a horrific drought and famine on the world? What were His purposes? What were His provisions?

_____

_____

_____

_____

6) What difficulties might Joseph have faced when he went so suddenly from the bottom of society to the top? What does this suggest about the importance of daily faithfulness to God?

_____

_____

_____

_____

_____

7) What are the qualities of a godly leader? Of a submissive follower? How do the two overlap?

_____

_____

_____

_____

8) When have you seen God use someone in authority to bring blessing in your life?

_____

_____

_____

PERSONAL RESPONSE

9) How well do you submit to authority figures? In what areas do you need to work on submission and respect toward authority?

_____

_____

_____

10) What practical lessons has the Lord taught you in times of hardship? How has He used those lessons in later situations?

_____

_____

_____

7

JOSEPH'S TESTS
Genesis 42:1–43:34

DRAWING NEAR

What are some ways in the past that you've "tested" a friendship to make sure it is genuine? What did your testing reveal?

_____

_____

_____

THE CONTEXT

Joseph had witnessed a remarkable reversal in life. After spending thirteen years as a slave and a prisoner, he had suddenly been elevated to second in command for all Egypt. For seven years after that time, he worked to gather up and store the abundance of grain in the land, knowing this time of plenty would soon end.

Just as God had said, a time of famine did indeed come to the region. It spread throughout Egypt, but because of Joseph's wise management, the inhabitants were fed. When people in other lands experiencing the same crisis heard there was food in Egypt, they began to travel there to secure grain. One of those who heard this news was none other than Jacob, the father of Joseph, and he sent his sons there to investigate.

When we left Joseph's brothers, they had just sold him into slavery and made it appear to their father as if he had been killed by a wild animal. Judah had then revealed his character by moving away from the family, marrying a Canaanite woman, violating the law of levirate marriage, and having sexual relations with a prostitute, who turned out to be his daughter-in-law. Clearly the situation had shifted in Joseph's favor, and from a human standpoint he would have had every reason to gloat at the fate of his brothers—or even seek revenge against them.

However, when Jacob's sons arrive in Egypt—and fail to recognize the man before them as their long-lost brother—we see no trace of resentment in Joseph. Instead, we find a man who only desires restoration. Of course, before this restoration can occur, Joseph must know if the attitude of his brothers' hearts has changed. Do they still harbor deadly hatred against him? Do they think at all about the crime they have committed against him? Do they harbor the same jealousy toward his full brother Benjamin, who is now their father's favorite?

To discover the answers to these questions, Joseph sets up a series of elaborate trials. During this study, we will look at these tests and see what they reveal to Joseph about the current state of his family. We will also see how Joseph, like Christ, chose to be obedient to God and fully trust in the Lord's sovereignty.

KEYS TO THE TEXT

Read Genesis 42:1–43:34, noting the key words and phrases indicated below.

THE BROTHERS HEAD TO EGYPT: Famine has gripped the land and spread throughout Canaan. There, Jacob and his family are facing a dire situation.

42:1. THERE WAS GRAIN IN EGYPT: The famine had grown so severe there was no food anywhere in Canaan. But, as we have seen, the Lord had provided enough to feed Egypt and Canaan by sending Joseph ahead to make preparations.

3. JOSEPH'S TEN BROTHERS WENT DOWN TO BUY GRAIN IN EGYPT: This was all according to God's plan, as He intended the same brothers who had

sent Joseph to Egypt to follow in his footsteps. The Lord's intention was to bring about reconciliation within Jacob's family, and this was a necessary first step.

4. JOSEPH'S BROTHER BENJAMIN: Benjamin and Joseph had both been born through Rachel. Jacob had not forgotten the tragic loss of Joseph, and he had no intention of losing his other favorite son.

5. AMONG THOSE WHO JOURNEYED: People were traveling to Egypt from all over Canaan, and probably beyond, because there was no food anywhere else. Joseph's brothers were merely a few men within a huge crowd that descended on Egypt. It took a miracle from the Lord for them even to encounter Joseph. This may also have given them a small taste of what it felt like to be sold into slavery.

BOWING BEFORE JOSEPH: Now, after twenty-two years, Joseph's prophetic dreams start to be fulfilled, as he witnesses his brothers bowing before him.

6. JOSEPH'S BROTHERS CAME: It is possible Joseph sat in attendance each day, perhaps elevated above the crowds. It may also have been the Lord's direct intervention to bring him to the market at just the right time for his brothers' appearance. Either way, this was no coincidence, for the Lord had foretold this event many years earlier.

AND BOWED DOWN BEFORE HIM: Here at last we find the literal fulfillment of Joseph's first dream. His second dream, in which his entire family bowed before him, had yet to be fulfilled (see Genesis 37:5–10).

7. HE ACTED AS A STRANGER TO THEM: This indeed was the case, since Joseph left Canaan at age seventeen and was now thirty-nine. His entire youth had been spent in Egypt, and his brothers could not truly say they knew him anymore.

SPOKE ROUGHLY TO THEM: This was the beginning of Joseph's plan of reconciliation, but it had to start with some rough treatment. Joseph could not simply pretend that the betrayal and attempted murder had never happened. Of course, the treatment Joseph gave to his brothers was far less rough than the treatment they had afforded to him many years earlier.

8. THEY DID NOT RECOGNIZE HIM: This is humorous in its understatement. Joseph had been a mere stripling when they had last seen him, and now he had grown into a strong, commanding adult. He had been an uneducated

shepherd lad, and now he stood before them in full splendor as the second-in-command of all Egypt. The brothers also assumed by this time that Joseph was dead. Given all this, it is hardly surprising that they did not recognize him!

> REFRESHING THEIR MEMORIES: *Joseph immediately sets about addressing the sins his brothers committed against him, working always toward reconciliation rather than revenge.*

9. YOU ARE SPIES: Joseph made this accusation as an excuse to speak to his brothers more closely and in private as an interrogator. He wanted to test their hearts to find out if they had repented of their wickedness toward him. He also longed for news of his father and brother Benjamin.

10. NO, MY LORD, BUT YOUR SERVANTS: This is further fulfillment of the prophecies the Lord had given through Joseph's dream (see Genesis 37:8). Finally, the brothers acknowledged—without even realizing it—that Joseph did indeed have dominion over them. It was important to the family's reconciliation for the brothers to confess openly that the Lord's prophecies had been fulfilled.

11. YOUR SERVANTS ARE NOT SPIES: The brothers had come to Egypt not expecting any trouble but merely wanting to buy food, as indeed everyone else in Canaan was doing. But to their dismay, they found themselves unexpectedly in grave danger. At this charge, they would have begun to fear for their lives, as spies would certainly have been put to death. In all this, they were again merely experiencing a small portion of what they had done to Joseph.

13. AND ONE IS NO MORE: This statement revealed to Joseph that his brothers had long ago given him up for dead, but that their consciences were still alive as to what they had done. It did not take much prompting for them to bring Joseph's "death" into the conversation, and this showed there was still hope for reconciliation.

> LOOKING FOR REPENTANCE: *Joseph wants to know that his brothers have repented of their sins against him, so he gives them an opportunity to demonstrate it.*

15. YOU SHALL BE TESTED: In fact, this was precisely what Joseph was doing—testing his brothers' hearts to find whether they had repented of their sins against him.

UNLESS YOUR YOUNGEST BROTHER COMES HERE: By focusing on Benjamin, Joseph forced his brothers to relive the events of the past, when they had betrayed their father's favorite son. Joseph was placing them in a position where they would have to determine how to treat Jacob's remaining favorite.

19. LET ONE OF YOUR BROTHERS BE CONFINED: Joseph had originally said that one brother would go to Canaan while the nine others remained, but here he reversed it. The latter plan was better for his purposes, as it forced the brothers to speak together on their way home. Joseph was confident that the subject of his betrayal would figure into their conversation.

20. BRING YOUR YOUNGEST BROTHER TO ME: Again, Joseph was compelling his brothers to address what they had done years before and giving them an opportunity to repent.

21. WE ARE TRULY GUILTY CONCERNING OUR BROTHER: Joseph could only offer the opportunity of repentance; he could not force his brothers to face their guilt. But the Spirit of God is always at work in His people, leading them to confess their sins and work toward reconciliation. This was precisely what was happening to Joseph's brothers at this point.

22. DID I NOT SPEAK TO YOU? Reuben had been the only brother who had attempted to save Joseph's life (see Genesis 37:21). Nevertheless, he had joined with his brothers in deceiving Jacob after selling Joseph into slavery (see verses 31–32), and he had done nothing to bring Joseph back from Egypt. Yet here he was suggesting that his guilt had been less than his brothers'! In the end, it would be Judah who came forth as the leader in the family.

24. HE TURNED HIMSELF AWAY FROM THEM AND WEPT: Joseph was not enjoying the process of putting his brothers through this anguish, but he felt it was necessary for full reconciliation to take place.

TOOK SIMEON: Joseph did not keep hostage Reuben, the firstborn, but Simeon, the oldest brother who had willingly participated in the crime against him.

A RANSOM FOR BENJAMIN: Joseph has sent his brothers to get Benjamin, but Jacob refuses to let him go. Both Reuben and Judah offer solutions, but only Judah's is acceptable.

28. WHAT IS THIS THAT GOD HAS DONE: When the brothers found inside one of the sacks the money with which they had purchased the grain, their conscience and fear of vengeance from God surfaced once again. Later,

upon discovering that *all* their money had been returned, their fear increased even more.

36. YOU WANT TO TAKE BENJAMIN: Jacob could not handle the prospect of losing his favored son, and he did not trust the brothers, who had already divested him of two other sons, by what he may have thought were their intrigues.

ALL THESE THINGS ARE AGAINST ME: The whole situation overwhelmed Jacob, who complained against his sons and would not release Benjamin.

37. REUBEN SPOKE TO HIS FATHER: Reuben was the firstborn and ordinarily would have been the leader for his brothers. But his earlier sin had removed him from that position in God's eyes, and his leadership had become ineffective.

KILL MY TWO SONS: The always-salutary Reuben generously made his father an offer that was easy for him to refuse—killing his grandsons.

38. MY SON SHALL NOT GO DOWN WITH YOU: Reuben's leadership failed.

DIFFICULT DECISION: In spite of Joseph's warning to the brothers not to return without Benjamin, Jacob is unwilling to part with his beloved son. It takes Judah's leadership to tip the scales.

43:3. JUDAH SPOKE TO HIM: Here we see that Judah was beginning to take up the role of the firstborn by taking leadership over his brothers.

SOLEMNLY WARNED US: The seriousness of Joseph's words portended failure for another mission to buy food unless the criterion he had set down was strictly met.

9. I MYSELF WILL BE SURETY FOR HIM: Reuben's offer of his two sons' lives as ransom was a bold suggestion, and he undoubtedly meant it as a firm sign of his commitment to protect Benjamin. But Judah offered a better ransom: his own life.

11. A LITTLE: Likely, this was a significant present because the family had little left. But there was no future at all past the little they had if they did not get grain in Egypt.

13. TAKE YOUR BROTHER ALSO: Jacob accepted his son Judah's offer over Reuben's.

14. MAY GOD ALMIGHTY GIVE YOU MERCY: Jacob's acquiescence to let Benjamin go ended with prayer for their safety and a cry of being a helpless

victim of circumstances. Pessimism had apparently set into Jacob's heart and deepened after the loss of Joseph.

23. YOUR GOD . . . HAS GIVEN YOU: This is an indication of Joseph's steward either having come to faith in God or having become familiar with how Joseph talked of his God. The brothers were so concerned about protesting their ignorance as to how the money had got back in their sacks that they missed the steward's clear reference to the God of Israel and the steward's own oversight of events in which he had played a part.

A LONG-LOST BROTHER: Joseph meets his brothers again, and this time Benjamin is with them. After such a long absence, he can hardly believe his eyes.

24. BROUGHT THE MEN INTO JOSEPH'S HOUSE: The brothers now returned to Egypt with Benjamin, just as Joseph had commanded.

25. THEY WOULD EAT BREAD THERE: Joseph deliberately kept the brothers in seclusion throughout this difficult process.

27. IS YOUR FATHER WELL: At each step along the way, Joseph betrayed his deep longing to be reconciled with his family. His brothers did not know who he was, and he yearned to reach the point where he could be reunited with them. It must have been a great joy for him to learn that his father was still alive.

28. PROSTRATED THEMSELVES: It is interesting to note how many times the brothers bowed before Joseph. This was the fulfillment of Joseph's prophetic dreams but also a sign that complete reconciliation had not yet taken place. Once the family was fully reconciled together, the brothers would no longer need to prostrate themselves before Joseph. The one exception came after Jacob's death, when the brothers fell into fear that Joseph would seek revenge.

29. IS THIS YOUR YOUNGER BROTHER: It had been more than two decades since Joseph had seen Benjamin, who was just a boy when they were separated.

30. JOSEPH MADE HASTE: Joseph made forgiveness and reconciliation with his brothers a top priority, which is why he did not waste any time in testing them.

WEEP . . . WEPT: Joseph wept frequently throughout the reconciliation process. These were probably mixed tears—tears of sorrow over the many years of separation mingled with tears of joy over the reunion.

32. THAT IS AN ABOMINATION TO THE EGYPTIANS: Exclusivism kept the Egyptians sensitive to the social stigma attached to sharing a meal table with foreigners.

33. THE FIRSTBORN ACCORDING TO HIS BIRTHRIGHT: To be seated at the table in birth order in the house of an Egyptian official was startling, and the brothers were astonished at how much he knew about them.

34. BENJAMIN'S SERVING WAS FIVE TIMES AS MUCH: The favoritism that Joseph showed to Rachel's son silently tested the brother's attitudes. Any longstanding envy, dislike, or animosity could not be easily masked—but none surfaced.

UNLEASHING THE TEXT

1) If you had been in Joseph's place, how would you have treated your brothers?

_____

_____

_____

_____

_____

2) How were the ransoms of Reuben and Judah different? What did their offers reveal about their respective characters?

_____

_____

_____

_____

_____

3) Why did Joseph meet with his brothers in private? What does this teach about forgiveness and reconciliation?

_____

_____

_____

_____

4) What steps were involved for the brothers to confess and repent of their sins against Joseph? What experiences helped them in that process?

_____

_____

_____

EXPLORING THE MEANING

God never forgets His promises. As a youth, God had given Joseph a prophetic dream. "There we were binding sheaves in the field. Then behold, my sheaf arose and also stood upright; and indeed your sheaves stood all around and bowed down to my sheaf" (Genesis 37:7). While we may question Joseph's wisdom in sharing that dream, there was never any question that God would cause it to come to pass.

God had taken Joseph through trials and sufferings so he would be ready when the time came for him to take authority. Without his leadership, not only would the people of Egypt have perished, but the citizens of Canaan would also have died—including Joseph's own family. Joseph accepted his situation as God's will, submitted himself to a burden of suffering, and as a result his life served a greater purpose.

"Therefore know that the LORD your God, He is God, the faithful God who keeps covenant and mercy for a thousand generations with those who love

Him and keep His commandments" (Deuteronomy 7:9). God always keeps His promises. Our role is to trust Him and act according to His will.

God tests us to determine what is in our hearts. Joseph's experiences undoubtedly tested his perseverance in believing the promises God had given him at a young age. At times he must have questioned what God was doing and why he had to endure such hardships. However, through it all Joseph never lost his faith in the Lord. His attitude as a slave, and later as a prisoner, reflects the humble state of his heart.

In the same way, the attitude Joseph displayed when he was in power reveals that his change in status had not affected his character. When he saw his brothers, he could have exerted his authority to take revenge against them. But instead, he used his power to bring restoration to all of Jacob's family. He tested his brothers, much as he had been tested in Egypt, to uncover what was in their hearts.

In John 3:17 we read, "God did not send His Son into the world to condemn the world, but that the world through Him might be saved." God's plan is never to condemn us but to save us, and He calls us to imitate that example by forgiving one another in love and humility. If we do not learn that lesson well, there is a good chance He will test us further to refine the attitude of our hearts. "Behold, I have refined you . . . I have tested you in the furnace of affliction" (Isaiah 48:10).

We will sow what we reap. Joseph allowed his brothers to experience just a bit of what he had experienced by throwing them into prison for three days. Then he purposefully put them in a difficult position by holding Simeon as a hostage and demanding they return with Benjamin. Finally, he increased their anxieties by placing the money they had paid for the grain in each of their sacks.

When the brothers returned home and told their father what had happened, they could do little to reassure him that Benjamin would be safe. After all, they could not reveal their past involvement in Joseph's disappearance and their deceitful cover-up if they wanted to have any hope of convincing Jacob to release his youngest son. The lesson wasn't lost on them. "Then they said to one another, 'We are truly guilty concerning our brother, for we saw the anguish of his soul when he pleaded with us, and we would not hear; therefore this distress has come upon us'" (Genesis 42:21).

Jesus said, "For with what judgment you judge, you will be judged; and with the measure you use, it will be measured back to you" (Matthew 7:2). Paul added, "Do not be deceived, God is not mocked; for whatever a man sows, that he will also reap" (Galatians 6:7). The brothers may have thought they had gotten away with their sin, but in the end God orchestrated events to reveal their guilt.

REFLECTING ON THE TEXT

5) Why did Joseph test his brothers? If someone repents of a sin against you, should you "test" that repentance or accept it at face value (see Matthew 18:21–22)?

_____

_____

_____

6) When Joseph told his brothers they must return with Benjamin, Reuben reminded them he had tried to save Joseph's life. How did his words represent truth and yet not serve as an admission of his guilt?

_____

_____

_____

7) What changed in Judah's heart to make him willing to be a ransom for Benjamin?

_____

_____

_____

8) What was the purpose of Joseph's giving Benjamin five times as much food as anyone else? What did his test reveal to him?

_____

_____

_____

_____

_____

PERSONAL RESPONSE

9) How has God tested you in the past to reveal what is in your heart? What did you learn about yourself through the process?

_____

_____

_____

_____

10) Why is it often so difficult to wait on God's timing to fulfill His promises? In what ways have you struggled with this in your life?

_____

_____

_____

_____

_____

8

A FAMILY RECONCILED
Genesis 44:1–45:15

DRAWING NEAR

What is a relationship you've had in your life that broke apart but later was mended? How did the process of reconciliation come about?

_____

_____

_____

THE CONTEXT

The word *reconciliation* comes from two Latin root words: (1) *re,* meaning "again," and (2) *concilare,* meaning "make friendly." Together, the word means "to become physically united once again." It suggests that something—a teacup, for example—has been broken in two and needs to be joined together again. This is a perfect word picture of the process of reconciliation: to rejoin two people who have been broken apart.

As we have seen, Joseph's family was shattered when his brothers sold him into slavery and told their father that he was dead. One of Joseph's foremost desires was to reunite his family—to pick up the pieces and glue them back into a single harmonious family. This was precisely what God desired as well.

The Lord calls His people to be reconciled, to work constantly at forgiving one another, and to keep "gluing together" fractured relationships. He has made His children into a single family, the unified body of Christ, and any division within that body is as painful as a broken bone. "For as the body is one and has many members, but all the members of that one body, being many, are one body, so also is Christ. For by one Spirit we were all baptized into one body—whether Jews or Greeks, whether slaves or free—and have all been made to drink into one Spirit" (1 Corinthians 12:12–13). The devil works to divide Christians, but the Holy Spirit works through us to bring harmony and reconciliation.

In the previous study, we examined how Joseph began the reconciliation process by putting his brothers through a series of tests to see if they felt any guilt about what they had done and to determine if they harbored any resentment toward Benjamin. In today's study, we will witness the conclusion of Joseph's tests and how they convinced him that a true change had occurred within his brothers. We will also examine how Joseph worked to reunite his family and will look for principles that can help us in the work of our own reconciliation.

KEYS TO THE TEXT

Read Genesis 44:1–45:15, noting the key words and phrases indicated below.

ANOTHER TEST: Joseph has one final test for his brothers to see just how far they will go to protect their father's favorite son, Benjamin.

44:2. MY CUP, THE SILVER CUP: Joseph's own special cup, also described as one connected with divination or "hydromancy" (interpreting the water movements), was a sacred vessel symbolizing the authority of his office as an Egyptian vizier. Mention of its superstitious nature and purpose need not demand that Joseph was an actual practitioner of pagan religious rites.

5. DIVINATION: The Egyptian practice of seeking to determine the will of the gods by examining and interpreting omens. Moses would later give strict injunctions to the Israelites not to imitate this practice (see Deuteronomy 18:9–12).

7. FAR BE IT FROM US: The brothers, facing a charge of theft, protested their innocence by pointing to their integrity in returning the money from the last trip, and then by declaring death on the perpetrator and slavery for themselves.

12. BEGAN WITH THE OLDEST: Again, Joseph displayed inside knowledge of the family, which should have signaled something to the brothers.

13. TORE THEIR CLOTHES: This is a well-known ancient Near Eastern custom to visibly portray the pain a person is experiencing. The brothers were in anguish that Benjamin might become a slave in Egypt. They had passed a second test of devotion to their youngest brother.

14. JUDAH AND HIS BROTHERS: It is interesting that Judah was now listed first, as the recognized leader in his family. The Lord had placed on him the responsibilities of the firstborn, and he had grown in godliness to the point that he fulfilled that role.

FELL BEFORE HIM: Again, Joseph's dream had become reality. But this time the brothers were pleading for mercy, both for their youngest brother, Benjamin, and for their father Jacob.

15. PRACTICE DIVINATION: Joseph, still disguising himself as an Egyptian official, permitted his brothers to think he could uncover the truth through this practice.

16. GOD HAS FOUND OUT THE INIQUITY OF YOUR SERVANTS: Judah had been confronted with the sins of the brothers and had repented. This was what Joseph was seeking: the repentance of his brothers and the reconciliation of his family.

17. HE SHALL BE MY SLAVE: Joseph was offering the brothers a chance to redeem themselves at the expense of their innocent brother. They had sinned in this way once before, and it must have been a tempting offer for them.

JUDAH INTERCEDES: The thought of betraying their father again is too much for Judah to take, and he makes a passionate plea on Benjamin's behalf.

18. JUDAH CAME NEAR TO HIM AND SAID: Judah, showing how his heart had changed, acknowledged the providence of God in uncovering the brothers' guilt. He did not indulge in any shifting of blame, even onto Benjamin.

LET YOUR SERVANT SPEAK A WORD: Judah would now make an eloquent and contrite plea for mercy, replete with reference to his aged father's delight in and doting on the youngest son and the fatal shock to him should Benjamin be lost.

31. HE WILL DIE: The brothers had not cared about Jacob's grief when they attempted to murder Joseph. But Judah and his brothers had since repented of that sin, and they were determined not to grieve their father any further.

33. LET YOUR SERVANT REMAIN INSTEAD OF THE LAD: Judah made good on his offer and was fully prepared to stand in the place of his brother, becoming a slave in Egypt.

THE REVELATION: *Joseph reveals himself and demonstrates the most important and final step in reconciliation: complete forgiveness.*

45:1. JOSEPH COULD NOT RESTRAIN HIMSELF: This took place immediately after Judah had offered himself in exchange for Benjamin's life. At last, Joseph could see that his brothers had truly repented of their sin. He was so moved by joy and yearning that he could no longer restrain his tears.

NO ONE STOOD WITH HIM: Joseph demonstrated that reconciliation is a private matter, not to be shared with an audience.

JOSEPH MADE HIMSELF KNOWN TO HIS BROTHERS: Imagine the powerful emotions that were surging in the hearts of the family at this moment. Joseph was overcome with joy at seeing his family again. Benjamin was probably overwhelmed with wonder to find that his long-dead brother was, in fact, alive—and a powerful ruler, besides. The other brothers probably felt a strong mixture of emotions, including awe at the fulfillment of Joseph's prophetic dreams and fear to be at his mercy.

3. THEY WERE DISMAYED: Literally, they were alarmed—and terrified. They fully expected that Joseph would desire revenge for their crimes against him, and they recognized he could exact that revenge with complete impunity. This allowed the brothers to experience the utter powerlessness and terror that Joseph had felt many years before. But in their fear, they did not understand the heart of their brother.

4. WHOM YOU SOLD INTO EGYPT: True reconciliation requires honesty from all parties. Joseph did not downplay what his brothers had done, nor

did he ignore their transgressions or try to gloss over them. They had sinned against him without cause, and all the brothers—including Joseph—needed to acknowledge that fact.

5. DO NOT THEREFORE BE GRIEVED OR ANGRY: The step of honest confession and admission of past sins must be followed with the step of full forgiveness. Forgiveness includes relinquishing any "right" or desire for revenge, just as Joseph freely relinquished his legal right and authority to exact revenge on his brothers.

THE BIG PICTURE: Joseph's final words to his brothers before sending them back to Canaan indicate his understanding of God's sovereign work in all of their lives.

5. GOD SENT ME BEFORE YOU TO PRESERVE LIFE: Joseph recognized it was the Lord who had sent him to Egypt. He understood that God had arranged the circumstances and used the deeds of men in order to further His own plans. Yet he also recognized that his brothers had sinned and needed to be reconciled with him.

6. THESE TWO YEARS: Joseph would have been thirty-nine years old by this time.

7. TO PRESERVE A POSTERITY: Joseph's words reflect his understanding of the Abrahamic covenant and its promise of a nation.

8. FATHER TO PHARAOH: This was a title that belonged to viziers. It designated a person who, though unrelated to Pharaoh, nevertheless performed a valuable function and held high position. In Joseph's case, this was "lord of all Egypt" (see verse 9). Note that a new and younger Pharaoh now reigned: Senusert III (c. 1878–1841 BC).

10. LAND OF GOSHEN: This area, located in the northeast section of the Egyptian delta region, was appropriate for grazing the herds of Jacob. More than 400 years later, during the time of the Exodus, the Jews would still live there (see Exodus 8:22; 9:26).

15. AFTER THAT HIS BROTHERS TALKED WITH HIM: Reconciliation was accomplished with much emotion, which clearly showed that Joseph held no grudges and had forgiven his brothers, evidencing the marks of a spiritually mature man. The family had been fully reconciled to one another, and they could once again speak together as brothers.

GOING DEEPER

Read the apostle Paul's words about reconciliation in 2 Corinthians 5:14–19, noting the key words and phrases indicated below.

> CHRIST'S SACRIFICE: *Paul shows how reconciliation with God is possible only because Jesus came to earth to pay the price for mankind's sin.*

5:14. THE LOVE OF CHRIST: Christ's loving, substitutionary death motivated Paul's service for Him. Paul's desire was to offer his life to the Lord.

ONE DIED FOR ALL: The preposition *for* indicates that Christ died "in behalf of," or "in the place of," all people. God's wrath against sin required death, but Jesus took that wrath and died in the sinner's place. Thus, He took away God's wrath, satisfied God's justice as a perfect sacrifice, and brought reconciliation between God and man.

15. HE DIED FOR ALL: Everyone who dies in Christ receives the benefits of His substitutionary death. Paul was overwhelmed with gratitude that Christ loved him and was so gracious as to make him a part of the "all" who died in Him.

16. ACCORDING TO THE FLESH: Since Paul's conversion, his priority had been to meet people's spiritual needs. He no longer evaluated people according to worldly standards.

> COMPLETE TRANSFORMATION: *Paul now explains what reconciliation with God looks like and how it profoundly changes the life of a believer in Christ.*

17. IN CHRIST: These two words comprise a brief but profound statement of the inexhaustible significance of the believer's redemption.

NEW CREATION: This describes something that is created at a qualitatively new level of excellence. The expression encompasses the Christian's forgiveness of sins paid for in Christ's substitutionary death on the cross.

OLD THINGS HAVE PASSED AWAY: After a person is regenerate, his old value systems, priorities, beliefs, loves, and plans are gone. Evil and sin are still present, but the believer sees them in a new perspective, and they no longer control him.

ALL THINGS HAVE BECOME NEW: The Greek grammar indicates this newness is a continuing condition of fact. The believer's new spiritual perception of everything is a constant reality for him, and he now lives for eternity, not temporal things.

> TRUE RECONCILIATION: *Paul explains to the believers that because God has reconciled Himself to them, they in turn need to seek reconciliation with others.*

18. MINISTRY OF RECONCILIATION: This speaks to the reality that God wills sinful men to be reconciled to Himself. God has called believers to proclaim the gospel of reconciliation to others. He wants Christians to accept the privilege of serving unbelievers by proclaiming a desire to be reconciled.

19. GOD WAS IN CHRIST: God by His own will and design used His Son, the only acceptable and perfect sacrifice, as the means to reconcile sinners to Himself.

RECONCILING THE WORLD: God initiates the change in the sinner's status in that He brings him from a position of alienation to a state of forgiveness and right relationship with Himself. This is the essence of the gospel.

IMPUTING: This is at the heart of the doctrine of justification. The moment the repentant sinner places wholehearted faith in Christ and His sacrificial death, God declares him righteous by covering him with the righteousness of Christ.

WORD OF RECONCILIATION: This indicates a true and trustworthy message, as opposed to a false or unsure one. In a world filled with false messages, believers have the solid, truthful message of the gospel.

UNLEASHING THE TEXT

1) How did Joseph's final test ultimately compel Judah to confess the sins he and his brothers had committed?

_____

_____

_____

2) In what ways did Judah change over the course of these passages? How did the Lord use his failures to teach him godly character?

_____

_____

_____

3) If you had been in the brothers' place, how would you have reacted when Joseph revealed his true identity?

_____

_____

_____

4) According to Paul, why must all believers in Christ seek reconciliation?

_____

_____

_____

EXPLORING THE MEANING

God's people should be reconciled with one another. Joseph never showed any inclination to get revenge on his brothers or on anyone else who had wronged him. His desire was just the opposite: to be reunited in complete unity and love with his family. The moment he had an opportunity, he set about working toward that reconciliation.

This is the example for all of God's people. We are to make reconciliation and forgiveness top priority in our lives. People do sin, and sometimes they will hurt us. Whether that is done intentionally or unintentionally, the pain is the same. Our job in such circumstances is to approach those who have offended us—not to confront them with their sin, but to offer forgiveness and reconciliation. This principle works in both directions, whether we are the ones offended or the ones who gave offense.

"If you bring your gift to the altar, and there remember that your brother has something against you, leave your gift there before the altar, and go your way. First be reconciled to your brother, and then come and offer your gift" (Matthew 5:23–24).

Forgiveness can be offered by one party alone, but reconciliation requires mutual effort. Joseph had forgiven his brothers for their sin long before he met them in Egypt. He had recognized it was God's plan that he be in Egypt in order to provide food for many people, and he had no desire to avenge himself for any sins against him. He was able to forgive regardless of his brothers' response.

However, he was not able to be fully reconciled with his family until his brothers acknowledged their sin and repented. This is a critical element in reconciliation: we must be willing to confess any action that might have hurt another person, and we must acknowledge that we have repented of that hurt—whether it was intentional or not.

This principle, like the previous one, works in both directions. We must be quick to be reconciled with others, regardless of whether we are the offending party or the offended party. "Confess your trespasses to one another, and pray for one another, that you may be healed. The effective, fervent prayer of a righteous man avails much" (James 5:16).

Our desire for reconciliation will serve as a strong testimony to the world. Joseph found it easier to forgive his brothers because he kept in mind that it was God's will for him to be in Egypt, regardless of what his brothers had intended. He lived with a constant recognition of God's sovereignty over the affairs of his life, which enabled him to quickly forgive those who sinned against him.

Joseph's brothers had a somewhat more difficult task in being reconciled because they did not fully understand this important concept. As we will see in the next study, when Jacob died they immediately became afraid again, thinking Joseph had complete power over their lives. Joseph had to remind them that he was not God, and that God alone had sovereignty. His model of forgiveness and desire for reconciliation served as a strong testimony to his brothers—and to us today.

People are watching us and will judge whether we truly live out what we profess to believe. If we faithfully obey God's Word and practice the ministry of reconciliation, they will be drawn to Christ. God's faithfulness to bless and care for His children will be visible to those around us—which will serve as a powerful witness to the world.

REFLECTING ON THE TEXT

5) What was required on Joseph's part to attain reconciliation? What was required on his brothers' part?

_____

_____

_____

_____

6) Why did Joseph want to be reconciled in the first place? What did he gain from it?

_____

_____

_____

7) How can you use Joseph's example to be reconciled with others in your life?

_____

_____

_____

_____

8) How can your efforts to forgive others and seek reconciliation serve as a powerful testimony to the work Jesus is doing in your life?

_____

_____

_____

_____

Personal Response

9) Is there a relationship in your life that needs to be reconciled? What will you do this week to make that happen?

_____

_____

_____

_____

10) Is there someone whom you need to forgive? Do you need to ask forgiveness of someone else? What steps will you take today to gain or offer forgiveness?

_____

_____

_____

_____

_____

9

RESCUING JACOB'S FAMILY

Genesis 45:16–47:12

DRAWING NEAR

What is a situation you have gone through that you can now look back on and see the ways in which God rescued you? How did He rescue you?

_____

_____

_____

THE CONTEXT

Now that the work of reconciliation had finally been accomplished, Joseph could set his mind on the joyful task of feeding his starving family. Yet he went far beyond merely providing food for them—he also provided them a new home in the richest part of Egypt and paid all the moving expenses to get his entire family situated there. For the first time, the descendants of Abraham would have permanent homes rather than nomadic tents. Those "permanent homes," it would turn out, would last some 400 years before the Lord would call His people back to Canaan.

Jacob was still living in Canaan during this period, dwelling in Hebron near the place where God had appeared to Abraham in Mamre (see Genesis

18). He had already buried his beloved wife Rachel (see Genesis 35:19), and it seems fairly likely that he had buried Leah as well (see Genesis 49:30–31). We are not told whether his concubines, Zilpah and Bilhah, were still alive at this point, though it is entirely possible that they were.

Joseph's second dream had included both his father and mother bowing before him in Egypt, so it is quite possible that some of Jacob's wives joined him on that trip. Regardless, Jacob was not lonely in Canaan, for his family had grown considerably. He was surrounded with his daughters-in-law and numerous grandchildren—as well as his beloved son, Benjamin.

The journey between Egypt and Hebron would take at least a week in each direction, and time would be required in Canaan to pack up and move the families and all their possessions back to Egypt. So Joseph provided many cartloads of food and provisions to nourish his family along the way—with far greater wealth awaiting them when they returned.

KEYS TO THE TEXT

Read Genesis 45:16–47:12, noting the key words and phrases indicated below.

> PHARAOH REJOICES: *Word comes to Pharaoh that Joseph's brothers have arrived in Egypt, and he is so glad that he sends for Jacob's entire family.*

45:16. SO IT PLEASED PHARAOH: The final seal of approval for Joseph's relatives to immigrate to Egypt came unsought from Pharaoh.

18. BRING YOUR FATHER AND YOUR HOUSEHOLDS: All of Joseph's brothers were with him in Egypt. Their own families had remained behind in Canaan, along with Jacob.

I WILL GIVE YOU THE BEST OF THE LAND OF EGYPT: The story of Joseph began with deep tragedy, and most of Joseph's life to this point had been spent in suffering. But it was God's hand that had led each step of the way, and His plan was to bring about great goodness for His children, not to prolong suffering.

YOU WILL EAT THE FAT OF THE LAND: Abraham's descendants had lived for several generations as nomads in Canaan, dwelling in tents and moving from place to place. More recently, they had been struggling just to survive during a time of terrible famine. Now, they suddenly found themselves taken out of Canaan to live in the world's wealthiest land—as honored guests in the best of that land.

LAST TRIP TO CANAAN: The brothers set forth on their last journey to Canaan to collect the remainder of their family. The people of Israel will not be back for many centuries to come.

22. BUT TO BENJAMIN: Joseph demonstrated special affection for his younger brother, Benjamin, because he was the only brother from his same mother, Rachel. This technically is not favoritism, as Joseph is merely one of the brothers rather than the father of the family, yet it is still worth noting that the other brothers did not exhibit any jealousy. This may indicate that true healing has taken place within the family.

24. SEE THAT YOU DO NOT BECOME TROUBLED ALONG THE WAY: The Hebrew word for *troubled* can mean "to tremble, rage, be agitated, be perturbed." This was a needed admonition, because they would have much to think about as they readied their confession to their father. Yet Joseph didn't want them to work themselves into fear concerning their sin against him, which had happened long before. It is interesting that he commanded them to "see to it," so as to make a deliberate effort not to dredge up the past. Joseph wanted his brothers' sin to be buried and forgotten.

26. JACOB'S HEART STOOD STILL: It was incredible to Jacob to be told that his son was still alive after he had firmly believed for so many years that Joseph was dead. It seemed too good to be true, but God's plans are always better than anything that we can hope for or imagine. "Now to Him who is able to do exceedingly abundantly above all that we ask or think, according to the power that works in us" (Ephesians 3:20).

JACOB HAS A VISION: Jacob takes his family from Bethel to Beersheba, where he stops to worship. While there, the Lord appears to him in a vision.

46:1. BEERSHEBA: Jacob's route to Egypt went through Beersheba, a notable site located about twenty-fives miles southwest of Hebron. Both

Abraham and Isaac had built altars there and publicly worshiped the Lord (see Genesis 21:33; 26:23–25).

2. IN THE VISIONS OF THE NIGHT: The Lord had given Jacob (also called Israel) a vision when he was in Bethel in which he saw a ladder or staircase ascending to heaven and God's angels moving up and down (see Genesis 28:12–15). The Lord promised Jacob in that vision that He would be with him wherever he went, that his descendants would be as innumerable as the dust of the earth, that they would spread throughout the earth, and that his offspring would inherit the land of Canaan.

3. DO NOT FEAR TO GO DOWN TO EGYPT: The Lord here reiterated His promise that He would be with Jacob, even in Egypt—a promise He had clearly kept even throughout the sufferings of Joseph. The Lord also repeated the promise: "Your descendants shall be as the dust of the earth; you shall spread abroad to the west and the east, to the north and the south" (Genesis 28:14).

4. I WILL ALSO SURELY BRING YOU UP AGAIN: The Lord had prophesied to Abraham that his descendants would be "strangers in a land that is not theirs," and that they would serve a foreign nation for 400 years before returning to Canaan (Genesis 15:13–16). He had prophesied to Jacob, "I am with you and will keep you wherever you go, and will bring you back to this land; for I will not leave you until I have done what I have spoken to you" (Genesis 28:15). He was now letting Jacob know that this journey into Egypt was the beginning of the fulfillment of those prophecies.

JOSEPH WILL PUT HIS HAND ON YOUR EYES: That is, Jacob would finish his days in peace and would die in the company of his beloved son Joseph.

ARRIVAL IN EGYPT: Joseph's intervention allows his family to safely make it to Egypt with their flocks and possessions, where they settle in the land of Goshen.

6. JACOB AND ALL HIS DESCENDANTS WITH HIM: Thus, Joseph's second dream was finally brought to pass, as his father and whole family came to Egypt and bowed themselves before his authority (see Genesis 37:9). This occurred sometime around 1875 BC.

8. THESE WERE THE NAMES: This genealogical register, which listed and totaled the sons per wife and handmaid, was enveloped by the statement that it recorded the sons/persons of Jacob who went to Egypt (see verses 8–27).

Ancient Near Eastern genealogies often included historical notes such as the ones given here—namely, the death of Er and Onan (see verse 12), and that Laban gave the handmaids Zilpah and Bilhah to his daughters (see verses 18, 25).

THE CHILDREN OF ISRAEL: This was the first time that Moses, the author of Genesis, referred to the family as a whole in this way, though the sons of Jacob had previously used the phrase "in Israel" (see Genesis 34:7).

26. SIXTY-SIX PERSONS: The total number of persons listed in verses 8–25 is seventy, from which Er, Onan, Manasseh, and Ephraim were deleted.

27. SEVENTY: Jacob, Joseph, Manasseh, and Ephraim were added to the sixty-six, for a total of seventy persons. The seventy-five people to which Stephen later referred in Acts 7:14 included an additional five people born in the land: two sons of Manasseh, two sons of Ephraim, and one grandson of the latter. These names were recorded in the Septuagint (the Greek translation of the Old Testament used by New Testament writers) but not in the Hebrew text.

28. SENT JUDAH BEFORE HIM: Once again, Jacob sent his son Judah to be the representative for the family, not Reuben.

31. I WILL GO UP AND TELL PHARAOH: Joseph's instructions about his preparatory interview with Pharaoh were designed to secure his relatives a place somewhat separate from the mainstream of Egyptian society. The social stigma regarding the Hebrews, who were also shepherds, played a crucial role in protecting Israel from intermingling and losing their identity in Egypt.

MEETING PHARAOH: Joseph completes the task of securing territory for his family by strategically arranging a meeting between Pharaoh and five family representatives.

47:1. THEY ARE IN THE LAND OF GOSHEN: Joseph, wise to Egyptian court procedures, informed Pharaoh of where he had located his family and then had five representatives of the family courteously request permission to reside there. In this way, Joseph paved the way for Pharaoh's confirmation and for his approval.

9. THE YEARS OF MY PILGRIMAGE: This was a fitting evaluation for Jacob to give, as neither he nor his fathers had actually possessed the land of Canaan. In addition, his years seemed few in contrast to those of his father (Isaac) and grandfather (Abraham) before him, who had visited Egypt long before him (180 and 175 years, respectively).

EVIL HAVE BEEN THE DAYS: Jacob, still overshadowed with pessimism, described his days as "evil," in the sense of the many toils, troubles, sorrows, distresses, and crises he had faced.

10. JACOB BLESSED PHARAOH: The aged patriarch's salutations pronounced, undoubtedly in the name of God, a benediction on Pharaoh Senusert III for his generosity and his provision of a safe place for his family. Although Senusert III had ascended to the throne before the famine ended, he honored his father's commitments.

11. JOSEPH SITUATED HIS FATHER AND HIS BROTHERS: Now that the meeting with Pharaoh had concluded successfully, Jacob was given the official seal of approval to settle in the land. Joseph's leadership found room for everyone.

IN THE BEST OF THE LAND: In an earlier study, we saw how Jacob's habitual favoritism made trouble for his sons. But here we see the positive aspect of that trait in his son Joseph, who did not hesitate to save the best for his own family.

IN THE LAND OF RAMESES: An alternative designation for Goshen, which Moses perhaps used here to more accurately describe the region for his contemporary readers. (The name was changed during the later rule of the powerful Ramses II.) This region is also called Zoan elsewhere (see Psalm 78:12, 43).

UNLEASHING THE TEXT

1) Why did Pharaoh rejoice so extravagantly when Joseph's brothers came to Egypt? What does this reveal about Joseph's character?

_____

_____

_____

2) If you had been in Jacob's place, how would you have responded when told that your son—whom you thought to be dead—was alive?

_____

_____

_____

3) Why did Joseph warn his brothers not to "become troubled" on their way back to Canaan? What does this reveal of Joseph's wisdom?

_____

_____

_____

4) What promise did God reiterate to Jacob when he passed through Beersheba? How was He leading Jacob through this vision?

_____

_____

_____

EXPLORING THE MEANING

God's prophetic words always come to pass. The Lord prophesied to Abraham that his descendants would one day journey to a foreign land where they would serve their masters for approximately 400 years, after which time they would return to Canaan. Abraham, however, never saw any part of that prophecy come to pass, nor did his son Isaac. In fact, it took several hundred years just for the first part to transpire, when Jacob's entire family finally moved to Egypt.

Abraham, Isaac, Jacob, and Joseph all knew the Lord's promises concerning His plans, but none of them knew the timetable or methods God would use to accomplish those plans. Yet they all lived their lives believing in the truth of His promises. The Lord used the wickedness of men to place His servant Joseph in the right position at the right time, yet that servant did not know, even in the midst of it, what the Lord was doing to bring about His prophecies.

God rarely tells us exactly how His prophetic words will come to pass. It is our part, as His children, to rest in faith that He will keep His Word. In the meantime, we are to remain faithful to the things that He has commanded us to do.

The Lord always provides for His people. The famine and drought in Egypt and Canaan were severe, and it is likely that many people died from its deprivations. Yet all of Jacob's household survived. In fact, they did more than survive—they *thrived* when the world around them was in want.

That famine did not catch God by surprise. He had ordained it as part of His strategy to move Israel into Egypt in preparation for their exodus into the Promised Land of Canaan. He saw all things that would transpire in the future, even to the end of time, and He had planned from before the beginning of time exactly how He would prove His faithfulness to His people.

Sometimes, however, His provision required that some of His people suffer. As we have seen, Joseph suffered grievously prior to being elevated to the leadership of Egypt, and it is likely that he wondered at times whether God had forgotten him. Jacob's continual pessimism in these passages indicates that he was also feeling the weight of the hardships he had endured. But the Lord had not forgotten Joseph, or Jacob, or any others in the family of Israel, and He proved it by providing for all their needs. He never failed to provide for His children.

We may experience sorrow for a time, but joy will certainly follow. The Lord permits sorrow and hardship to enter the lives of His children from time to time. When we are in the midst of those trials, it can be hard to see any joy that might result. Yet the Lord proved His sovereignty over all the circumstances of Joseph's life, and He is still sovereign today over the affairs of our lives.

The Lord permits both blessings and sorrows to enter our lives for the express purpose of making us more like Christ. Paul pointed to this fact when he wrote, "And we know that all things work together for good to those who love God, to those who are the called according to His purpose. For whom He foreknew, He also predestined to be conformed to the image of His Son, that He might be the firstborn among many brethren" (Romans 8:28–29).

For this reason, we can agree with James when he writes, "My brethren, count it all joy when you fall into various trials, knowing that the testing of your faith produces patience. But let patience have its perfect work, that you may be perfect and complete, lacking nothing" (James 1:2–4). We can also say with the psalmist, "Sing praise to the LORD, you saints of His, and give thanks at the remembrance of His holy name. For His anger is but for a moment, His favor is for life; weeping may endure for a night, but joy comes in the morning" (Psalm 30:4–5).

REFLECTING ON THE TEXT

5) If you had been one of Joseph's ten brothers, how would you have reacted to Joseph's generosity?

_____

_____

_____

_____

6) How might the ten brothers have felt as they journeyed back to Canaan? How might they have felt when explaining to Jacob what really happened to Joseph?

_____

_____

_____

_____

7) List below the major circumstances and events the Lord used in Joseph's life to bring about this great provision for his family. What does this reveal about His sovereignty?

_____

_____

_____

_____

8) List below some prophecies of Scripture that have not yet been completely fulfilled. How should these prophecies affect your life today?

_____

_____

_____

PERSONAL RESPONSE

9) When have you seen the Lord's generous provision in your life? When have you struggled during times of deprivation?

_____

_____

_____

10) Are you building your life today on the promises of God? Do you truly believe what the Bible says concerning the future? Why or why not?

_____

_____

_____

10

JACOB FINISHES IN FAITH
Genesis 47:13–48:22

DRAWING NEAR

What legacy do you want to leave behind for your friends and family?

_____

_____

_____

THE CONTEXT

We now come to the height of the famine in Egypt, after Joseph has settled his family in the land of Goshen. In the course of just a few years, the entire population will go from exchanging their money for grain, to exchanging their livestock for grain, to exchanging their lands—and thus their freedom—for grain. While this method sounds harsh, it was beneficial to the Egyptians because their food supply became Pharaoh's responsibility.

As the famine comes to an end, so does Jacob's time on earth. He has grown frail, and his eyesight has failed. He senses that his days are growing short, and he wants to pass on his fatherly blessing to his children. Interestingly, he begins with the sons of Joseph. Part of this first blessing is to adopt Joseph's sons as his own, rather than to view them as his grandsons. This is a mark of high favor and esteem, since it confers to Joseph's sons the full inheritance rights of him and his brothers. It effectively triples Joseph's family inheritance by conferring a share on his sons as well as himself.

In a final twist, God has Jacob reverse the blessing on Joseph's two sons. In doing so, He repeats a pattern we find throughout Genesis of conferring the blessing on later-born offspring. We first witnessed this pattern with Abel, whose sacrifice God respected over his older brother Cain's. Later, the Lord would consider Isaac to be the chosen son of promise, even though he was the second-born son of Abraham. This continued with Jacob, who deceived his father to receive the blessing of the firstborn, and then Jacob's son Judah became the primary carrier of God's blessing when Reuben committed a sin that made him unfit to receive the privilege.

In this study, we will examine Joseph's leadership during the years of the great famine and look more closely at Jacob's blessings to Joseph's two sons.

KEYS TO THE TEXT

Read Genesis 47:13–48:22, noting the key words and phrases indicated below.

EVERYTHING COLLAPSES: The people of Egypt and Canaan run out of food, the monetary systems collapse, and the whole world is in danger of starvation. Yet Joseph remains firm.

47:13. THERE WAS NO BREAD IN ALL THE LAND: The entire known world of Joseph's day continued to suffer from the devastating drought and famine. Evidently, by this point Joseph had instituted some form of rationing system.

14. JOSEPH BROUGHT THE MONEY INTO PHARAOH'S HOUSE: One of the traits of Joseph's life was faithfulness. He remained faithful to his master, first in Potiphar's house, and then as Pharaoh's trusted minister. This is another important aspect of leadership: a good leader will first be a good follower, faithful to his superiors.

15. THE MONEY FAILED: This famine was so extreme that it caused a collapse of Egypt's monetary system. Yet even this extremity did not cause Joseph's leadership to collapse, as it has at other times and places in history. Joseph overcame the danger by instituting a bartering system.

17. HE FED THEM WITH BREAD IN EXCHANGE FOR ALL THEIR LIVE-STOCK: First, Joseph accepted animals in exchange for grain. While this may sound harsh, we must remember that the livestock would not have survived otherwise. If there was no food for the people, there was certainly none for the animals.

19. BUY US AND OUR LAND: After the animals ran out, the people were desperate enough to exchange their land for food. The famine had thus led to the entire collapse of the governmental order, yet God remained with Joseph during this dreadful ordeal. The nation of Egypt—along with Pharaoh's throne—were kept intact because of Joseph's leadership, and his leadership was sound because he attended to God's Word.

20. THE LAND BECAME PHARAOH's: Eventually, Pharaoh owned all the land, except what was owned by the priests. The system of government Joseph instituted resembled the feudal system in Europe during the Middle Ages.

WISE MANAGEMENT: *As the famine continues, Joseph creates a policy of moving the people to the cities and institutes an income tax on the land.*

21. HE MOVED THEM INTO THE CITIES: Here we find yet another major change that has caused changes in governmental authorities at other times, as Joseph changed the demographics of the entire nation of Egypt.

24. YOU SHALL GIVE ONE-FIFTH TO PHARAOH: Whatever may have been the land-tenure system at that time, some private land ownership did at first exist, but finally, as in a feudal system, all worked their land for Pharaoh. The landed nobility lost out and declined during these major social reforms carried out under Senusert III. This is the first record in Scripture of a national income tax, and the amount was twenty percent. Later, after the exodus, God would prescribe tithes for Israel as national income taxes to support the theocracy (see Malachi 3:10), and He would use a national income tax to send Joseph and Mary to Bethlehem, where His Son was born (see Luke 2:1).

25. YOU HAVE SAVED OUR LIVES: Throughout all these tumultuous changes, the people remained loyal to Joseph—and thus to Pharaoh. Whatever the gain to Pharaoh, the people obviously understood that Joseph had not enriched himself at their expense. This alone is a testimony to the strength of Joseph's leadership.

27. **Israel dwelt in the land of Egypt**: The Lord did these things to bless Joseph, but His purposes went well beyond that. He had intended for Abraham's descendants to live in Egypt (see Genesis 15:13), and this was His way of moving Israel's entire family there. God's purposes in our personal lives include our own blessings, but His plans are always far bigger than we can see.

Joseph's Vow: When Jacob feels that his time on earth is coming to an end, he calls for Joseph and asks to be buried back in his homeland.

27. **grew and multiplied**: Jacob was witness to this increase in population for seventeen years. In this way, he was given a glimpse of God's promise to Abraham, Isaac, and himself in the process of being fulfilled.

29. **your hand under my thigh**: An ancient Near Eastern custom by which an intimate touch affirmed an oath.

do not bury me in Egypt: With the customary sign of an oath in that day, Joseph sincerely promised to bury Jacob, at his request, in the family burial cave in Canaan.

Jacob Adopts Two Sons: Jacob now has Joseph present his two sons, Ephraim and Manasseh, before him—and he adopts them as his own sons.

48:1. **Manasseh and Ephraim**: These were Joseph's sons, born in Egypt. Manasseh means "causes [me] to forget." Ephraim means "double fruit." Manasseh was the older of the boys.

3. **God Almighty appeared to me at Luz**: This is a reference to the events in Genesis 28:10–22. At that time, Jacob changed the name from Luz to Bethel.

5. **your two sons . . . are mine**: Jacob, in gratitude for Joseph's great generosity and preservation of God's people, formally adopted Manasseh and Ephraim on a par with Joseph's brothers in their inheritance. This elevated them to the status of firstborn sons rather than grandsons. In this way, Jacob gave Ephraim the full birthright that would have fallen to Reuben, had he not committed his grievous sin.

6. YOUR OFFSPRING WHOM YOU BEGET AFTER THEM SHALL BE YOURS: That is, Joseph's future children would receive their inheritance from him—his third son would be treated as his firstborn, and so forth.

8. WHO ARE THESE? It is possible that Jacob was remembering the terrible trick he had played on his own blind father, pretending to be his older brother in order to receive Esau's inheritance (see Genesis 27).

9. I WILL BLESS THEM: Jacob did indeed grow into a godly man of faith. He was more like his grandfather, Abraham, than he had been in his earlier life. Jacob was now passing on the godly blessing, just as his father Isaac had done for him.

10. HE COULD NOT SEE: Jacob, a bent and aged man, was evidently leaning on his staff. His physical eyes could no longer see, but the Lord had opened his spiritual eyes. The author of Hebrews would later develop this theme when he wrote, "By faith Jacob, when he was dying, blessed each of the sons of Joseph, and worshiped, leaning on the top of his staff" (Hebrews 11:21).

11. GOD HAS ALSO SHOWN ME YOUR OFFSPRING: Jacob recognized that God's hand had been guiding all the events in his life, even during the times when it appeared as though the Lord had abandoned him. God had led him through times of sorrow, yet in the end He had blessed Jacob more greatly than he could have imagined.

JACOB BLESSES HIS NEW SONS: *Jacob now places his hands of blessing on Ephraim and Manasseh—but he deliberately reverses their birth order.*

13. EPHRAIM WITH HIS RIGHT HAND TOWARD ISRAEL'S LEFT HAND: Joseph attempted to arrange things so the blessing of Jacob would be properly administered—according to human expectations. But God's will always overrides human efforts. It was in God's plan to give the firstborn status to the younger son, just as He had done with Jacob.

14. GUIDING HIS HANDS KNOWINGLY: Jacob deliberately crossed his hands, placing his right hand on the younger son and reversing the arrangement Joseph anticipated. Thus, Jacob's blessing became a word of prophecy concerning Ephraim, anticipating that Ephraim would become the more influential of the two sons. The name Ephraim eventually became a substitute name for the nation of Israel (see, for example, Isaiah 7).

15. BLESSED JOSEPH: Jacob, with his hands on the sons' heads, uttered the prayer-wish for Joseph, which indicated by his wording that these two would be taking his son's place under Abraham and Isaac.

16. WHO HAS REDEEMED ME FROM ALL EVIL: This is the first mention in Scripture of God as Redeemer, Deliverer, or Savior.

17. IT DISPLEASED HIM: As we have seen in previous studies, the birthright of the firstborn son included the father's greatest blessing, as well as a larger share in the inheritance. The Lord, however, sometimes changed the order of precedence.

HE TOOK HOLD OF HIS FATHER'S HAND: When Joseph attempted to correct his father's mistake, he learned that Jacob knew exactly what he was doing.

19. HIS YOUNGER BROTHER SHALL BE GREATER: Ephraim did indeed become the dominant tribe of the ten northern tribes of Israel.

21. GOD WILL . . . BRING YOU BACK: In this way, the dying Jacob gave voice to his undying trust in God's taking his descendants back to Canaan.

22. I TOOK FROM THE HAND OF THE AMORITE: Jacob's history does not record any conquest of Amorite land. He did purchase property from the children of Hamor (see Genesis 33:19), but that was not by conquest. It appears that at some time this military event had actually occurred, but for some unknown reason it finds no other mention in God's revelation.

UNLEASHING THE TEXT

1) How did God use Joseph to guide both the Egyptians and Jacob's family through the height of the famine?

_____

_____

_____

_____

_____

2) Why did Jacob ask Joseph to bury him in his homeland? What was the significance of this request in light of the covenant God had made with Abraham?

_____

_____

_____

3) How did Jacob's decision to adopt Manasseh and Ephraim as his own sons reveal his understanding of God's provision for his entire family?

_____

_____

_____

4) Why did Jacob cross his arms when blessing Joseph's sons? Why did Joseph attempt to correct his father in this act?

_____

_____

_____

EXPLORING THE MEANING

Christians are adopted as sons of God through Christ Jesus. Jacob adopted Joseph's two sons as his own, and they received a full share of Israel's inheritance along with their father, Joseph. In an extended sense, this provides us with a picture of God's great plan of adoption, establishing each man and woman who accepts His Son's salvation as a child of God.

The picture is imperfect, however, because Joseph's sons were still part of Jacob's family—while we had no part in the family of God apart from Christ.

We had no hope of seeing God's face, never mind any hope of inheriting eternal life in His presence. But His Son, Jesus, has shared with us His own inheritance, making us part of the family of God and children who have full access to the Father.

"When the fullness of the time had come, God sent forth His Son, born of a woman, born under the law, to redeem those who were under the law, that we might receive the adoption as sons. And because you are sons, God has sent forth the Spirit of His Son into your hearts, crying out, 'Abba, Father!' Therefore you are no longer a slave but a son, and if a son, then an heir of God through Christ" (Galatians 4:4–7).

God chooses the foolish things of the world to confound the wise. When Joseph presented his sons to their grandfather, he arranged them so that Manasseh, the eldest, was placed under Jacob's right hand. Throughout Scripture the right-hand side is considered the place of greatest honor and blessing, so this was an appropriate action for Joseph to take. Yet God confounded that logic by prompting Jacob, though blind, to cross his arms so that his right hand fell on Ephraim.

In 1 Corinthians 1:27, Paul writes, "God has chosen the foolish things of the world to put to shame the wise, and God has chosen the weak things of the world to put to shame the things which are mighty." God will use anything or anyone to fulfill His purposes on this earth, regardless of whether they fit our ideas of what is proper or whether they violate our concepts of the established norm.

We see this clearly in the genealogy of Christ given in Matthew 1:1–17. Of the four women listed, one was a prostitute (Rahab), one conceived a child by tricking her father-in-law (Tamar), one was a Gentile from a pagan nation (Ruth), and one committed adultery (Bathsheba). This is not the family tree we would expect to see in the bloodline of the Messiah, but it shows how God uses all people for His purposes, regardless of their birth order, past actions, class, or occupations.

"In truth I perceive that God shows no partiality. But in every nation whoever fears Him and works righteousness is accepted by Him" (Acts 10:34–35).

We must run the race in faith—and finish in faith. Jacob was not perfect by any means, and there were certainly times when he failed to live by faith. As a young man, he swindled his brother out of his birthright. He lied to his father to receive the family blessing. He was crafty in his dealings with his uncle Laban. He played favorites with his wives and his sons, which led to much suffering in his family. Yet for all his faults, Jacob ended his days with a deep faith in God.

Jesus would later tell a parable about a man who sowed seed in a field (see Matthew 13:1–9). Some of the seed did not produce a harvest because it fell by the wayside, or on rocky soil, or among thorns, and did not finish what had been started. But some of the seed fell on good soil, finished its purpose, and grew into a rich harvest. This is an important principle for God's people to keep in mind: we must live by faith, and we must *continue* to live by faith as long as the Lord chooses to keep us on earth.

Paul compared the Christian life to a person running a footrace (see 1 Corinthians 9:24–27). The runner might begin the race with great zeal, but he cannot hope to win the race unless he *finishes* well. We see this in the life of Joseph and others we have studied in the book of Genesis. They may have stumbled along the way, but the general pattern of their lives was that of living by faith.

REFLECTING ON THE TEXT

5) Do you think Joseph was acting justly with the people when he took their money, livestock, and land in exchange for food?

_____

_____

_____

6) Why did the Egyptians accept these terms? Why do you think Joseph was able to make these reforms and still find favor with the people?

_____

_____

_____

111

7) Why did Jacob, as one of his last acts on earth, remind Joseph of the promises God had made to him? Why was that important for Joseph to hear?

_____

_____

_____

8) How did Jacob finish his race in faith? How does this prove that God can use anyone to fulfill His purposes?

_____

_____

_____

PERSONAL RESPONSE

9) Do you think of yourself as an adopted child of God? How might this attitude influence your life in the coming week?

_____

_____

_____

10) What is more important to your self-evaluation: the opinions of others or the opinion of God? Why? How does this play out in your daily life?

_____

_____

_____

11

THE SOVEREIGNTY OF GOD

Genesis 49:1–50:21

DRAWING NEAR

What are some specific blessings that God has given to you? What are some specific ways you have seen Him correct a misstep?

_____

_____

_____

THE CONTEXT

Jacob's last act recorded in the book of Genesis is to gather his twelve sons together and pronounce a blessing on each one. These blessings are not simple benedictions but specific prophecies concerning the future tribes of Israel—the future descendants of each son. Though blind, Jacob sees each son with true and accurate vision. He recognizes their strengths and areas of obedience, but also their weaknesses and sins. His words of prophecy will be fulfilled in the later history of the nation of Israel.

Jacob's final blessing on his sons reflects the sovereignty of God at work. Reuben, Simeon, and Levi are all passed over because of their sins, while Judah, the fourth-born, is told the scepter will not depart from him. This is not an arbitrary or random act, for ultimately we know that Jesus, the king of kings, descended from Judah's bloodline.

Furthermore, by the end of Joseph's story, it becomes clear that while his life was filled with events that seemed arbitrary and out of his control—and indeed *were* out of his control—they were never out of God's control. The Lord had a large-scale plan to take His chosen nation into Egypt, and that plan included using the evil intentions of Joseph's brothers to send him there ahead of the family. Nothing could alter this sovereign plan of God from coming to pass.

In today's study, we will see how the brothers have still not grasped this truth even after all the events that have transpired. With the death of their father, they begin to worry that Joseph will go back on his word and seek to repay their evil. Joseph has to set them straight and show them the bigger plan God has in store for His people.

KEYS TO THE TEXT

Read Genesis 49:1–50:21, noting the key words and phrases indicated below.

> REUBEN, SIMEON, AND LEVI'S BLESSING: *Jacob now calls his own sons before him and pronounces prophetic blessings on them and their descendants. His words for his first three sons portend unpleasant things to come for their tribes.*

49:1. JACOB CALLED HIS SONS: Jacob's recorded blessings in this section of Scripture, which were highly poetic, portrayed the history of the tribes that would descend from each son. The order of blessing did not follow any discernible pattern.

3. REUBEN, YOU ARE MY FIRSTBORN: Jacob began his blessing with his firstborn son, which would ordinarily have been natural. But in this case, he started by stating plainly that his firstborn son had lost his rights due to his grievous sin.

MY MIGHT AND THE BEGINNING OF MY STRENGTH: In this heart-breaking statement, Jacob reminded Reuben what special blessings and influence were once his by right—all of which he had forever lost. He had followed the pattern of Esau, who gave up his birthright in exchange for a bowl of soup (see Genesis 25:21–34).

4. UNSTABLE AS WATER: The Hebrew phrase is literally "frothy water." Reuben was like a pot of boiling water—dangerous and unstable.

YOU WENT UP TO YOUR FATHER'S BED: "And it happened, when Israel dwelt in that land, that Reuben went and lay with Bilhah his father's concubine; and Israel heard about it" (Genesis 35:22).

5. SIMEON AND LEVI ARE BROTHERS: That is, they are two of a kind.

INSTRUMENTS OF CRUELTY ARE IN THEIR DWELLING PLACE: The brothers had plundered the Hivites after slaughtering the family of Shechem, and they probably still had some of that plunder in their possession (see Genesis 34).

7. DIVIDE THEM IN JACOB AND SCATTER THEM IN ISRAEL: Simeon became the smallest tribe in Israel (see Numbers 26:14) and eventually shared territory with Judah (see Joshua 19:1–9). His descendants were omitted from Moses' final blessing (see Deuteronomy 33). Levi was scattered throughout Israel in the sense his descendants did not receive any part of the Promised Land. Yet the Lord showed His grace when Levi's descendants remained loyal to Him by making them the priestly tribe in Israel (see Exodus 32:26). The Levites were the only people in Israel who could become priests—and, as such, they were spread throughout the nation.

JUDAH'S BLESSING: *The tone of Jacob's blessing changes when he comes to Judah, whose tribe will ultimately become the largest in the nation of Israel.*

8. JUDAH, YOU ARE HE WHOM YOUR BROTHERS SHALL PRAISE: Judah's brothers would "praise" him in the sense of recognizing his authority as leader of the family.

YOUR FATHER'S CHILDREN SHALL BOW DOWN BEFORE YOU: This was fulfilled in David, Solomon, and their dynasty—Israel's great kings. It will ultimately be fulfilled, however, in Christ, before whom *every* knee shall bow (see Romans 14:11; Philippians 2:10–11).

10. UNTIL SHILOH COMES: This probably refers to Christ, who is called the "Lion of the tribe of Judah" (Revelation 5:5).

11. BINDING HIS DONKEY TO THE VINE: This poetically describes a time of great prosperity, when people will tie a donkey to a choice vine and allow it to eat freely because of the abundance. Wine will be as plentiful as water,

and people will enjoy good health and contentment (verse 12, "eyes . . . darker than wine; teeth whiter than milk"). This is probably a prophecy concerning the millennial kingdom of Christ.

> ZEBULUN THROUGH DAN: *Jacob utters words of prophecy concerning the remaining tribes of Israel, many of which will be fulfilled during the time of the judges.*

13. A HAVEN FOR SHIPS: The descendants of Zebulun did not live near the Mediterranean Sea, but their territory benefited from an important trade route that was used by sea traders in Canaan.

14. A STRONG DONKEY: The name Issachar means "man of wages." The descendants of Issachar would become a strong and industrious tribe.

16. DAN SHALL JUDGE HIS PEOPLE: The name Dan means "judge." This prophecy would be fulfilled during the period of the judges.

17. BITES THE HORSE'S HEELS: This prophecy probably points to Samson, whose exploits caused the Philistines to rise up against the people of Israel and led to the nation's finally taking control of Canaan under King David.

18. I HAVE WAITED FOR YOUR SALVATION, O LORD: Jacob's impassioned cry expressed hope for the tribe of Dan when salvation came to Israel—but Dan was ultimately omitted from the list of tribes in Revelation 7:4–8.

20. HE SHALL YIELD ROYAL DAINTIES: The tribe of Asher settled in the agriculturally rich coastal region north of Carmel. They provided gourmet delights for the kings of Israel.

21. A DEER LET LOOSE: The speed and agility of a deer marked the military prowess of the tribe of Naphtali (see Judges 4:6; 5:18).

HE USES BEAUTIFUL WORDS: The song of Deborah and Barak would later demonstrate the tribe's eloquence (see Judges 5).

23. ARCHERS HAVE BITTERLY GRIEVED HIM: We have seen already how Joseph's life was filled with enemies, and how people even dear to him sought his harm. Yet Joseph "remained in strength . . . by the hands of the Mighty God" (verse 24).

27. BENJAMIN IS A RAVENOUS WOLF: The warlike nature of the small tribe of Benjamin became well known, as exhibited in their archers and slingers (see, for example, Judges 20:15–16).

JACOB'S DEATH: Jacob issues a final request concerning his place of burial, and then the aged patriarch breathes his last.

29. I AM TO BE GATHERED TO MY PEOPLE: As we will see, these dying instructions from Jacob would be fully carried out by his sons (see Genesis 50:12–13).

31. THERE I BURIED LEAH: Jacob finally bestowed honor on Leah by requesting to be buried alongside her, as were his fathers. He did not request burial alongside Rachel, his beloved wife.

33. JACOB . . . BREATHED HIS LAST: This took place around 1858 BC.

GATHERED TO HIS PEOPLE: A euphemism for death, but also an expression of personal continuance beyond death, which denoted a reunion with previously departed friends.

50:2. PHYSICIANS TO EMBALM HIS FATHER: Joseph summoned medical men rather than religious embalmers to avoid the magic and mysticism associated with their practices.

3. FORTY DAYS WERE REQUIRED: In Egypt, mummifying was a forty-day process, which included gutting the body, drying it, and wrapping it.

4. WHEN THE DAYS OF HIS MOURNING WERE PAST: Once normal embalming and mourning had been properly observed according to Egyptian custom, Joseph was free to seek permission to conduct a funeral in Canaan.

9. THERE WENT UP WITH HIM BOTH CHARIOTS AND HORSEMEN: Out of respect for Joseph, a substantial escort accompanied him and all his relatives into the land of Canaan.

GOD MEANT IT FOR GOOD: After Jacob's death, the brothers' guilty consciences reassert themselves and cause them to underestimate the genuineness of Joseph's forgiveness.

14. AFTER HE HAD BURIED HIS FATHER: After Joseph and his brothers buried their father in Canaan, they all returned to their new homes in Goshen.

15. PERHAPS JOSEPH WILL HATE US: Joseph's brothers suddenly began to wonder whether Joseph had been kind to them solely to please their father. With Jacob out of the way, would he now remember all the evil they had done to him years before? Their sin against their brother was coming back in the form of fear and false expectations. They expected Joseph to behave toward them as they had behaved toward him.

FOR ALL THE EVIL WHICH WE DID TO HIM: Here we see that the brothers had indeed repented of their sins toward Joseph, as they recognized and freely confessed their wicked deeds.

17. JOSEPH WEPT WHEN THEY SPOKE TO HIM: This is a deeply moving passage, and we can understand the mixture of grief and joy Joseph must have felt. He was joyful his brothers had repented but grieved they did not understand how much he loved them.

19. AM I IN THE PLACE OF GOD? Joseph recognized that everything he had experienced was under the direct control of God. The Lord had moved him from his father's family into slavery, from slavery into prison, and from prison to the house of Pharaoh—specifically because He had a plan for Jacob's descendants. Joseph realized that God was unfolding His plan for His people, and that plan extended far beyond the lives of Jacob's immediate family.

20. YOU MEANT EVIL AGAINST ME; BUT GOD MEANT IT FOR GOOD: Here is the crux of Joseph's attitude toward the many evils that were done against him: they meant it for evil, but God meant it for good. When we imitate this attitude, we spare ourselves a great deal of suffering during times of hardship and can fully cooperate with whatever plan the Lord is unfolding through our lives.

TO SAVE MANY PEOPLE ALIVE: Joseph also recognized that God's plan for his life was merely part of a larger plan for the entire family. Indeed, it was a small part of God's huge scheme for making redemption available to the entire human race. The Lord does work out the details of our lives for our own blessing, making us more and more like His Son, but His plans extend far beyond us. The sovereignty of God is too large for the human mind to comprehend.

UNLEASHING THE TEXT

1) What stands out to you in Jacob's blessings? What themes do you find?

_____

_____

_____

_____

2) Why is the blessing on Judah so significant? How does his blessing point to the coming of Jesus, the Messiah?

_____

_____

_____

3) Why did Jacob repeat the request he made to Joseph to be buried back in Canaan? What additional items did he add to the request that he made to all his sons?

_____

_____

_____

4) How did Joseph's brothers show that they didn't understand God's sovereignty? What finally helped them learn that lesson?

_____

_____

_____

EXPLORING THE MEANING

God knows the truth about our character. Jacob's blessings on his sons can seem startling in their frankness, but he was speaking truth about the sons' characters. He did not gloss over the sins of Reuben or Simeon, yet he also saw areas of strength and virtue. He spoke truth that sometimes hurt and sometimes encouraged.

The Lord also sees the truth about our lives—the areas of sin and weakness as well as the areas of strength and obedience. The Lord's perspective on our character is the only *true* perspective, whatever other people may think. There are times when we might think a character flaw does not show to others; perhaps we have even blinded ourselves to it. But the Lord still sees what is true. Conversely, others may never know of the small areas of faithfulness that are done in secret—but the Lord knows.

The other side of this principle is that God looks on His children through the blood of Christ, and He sees us as spotless and immeasurably precious. When the Father looks at us, He sees His Son—and we are "accepted in the Beloved" (Ephesians 1:6). We have been redeemed from sin, yet we are still sinful human beings. The Lord does see the sinfulness in our lives, yet He ultimately views us as His adopted sons—full heirs of all the promises of Christ. Our sinfulness does not negate our righteous standing before God, and we can never lose our adoption into His family.

The actions of men cannot frustrate the purposes of God. Joseph's brothers envied the plans God had for him, and they conspired together to frustrate those plans. They deliberately set out to prevent him from ruling over them, first by planning to murder him and then by selling him into slavery. From a human perspective, it would certainly seem that God's plans had been thwarted when Joseph was led away in chains.

It turned out, however, that their wicked deeds merely advanced God's plan for Joseph's life. Joseph and his family could not see that at the time, but God knew exactly where He wanted Joseph at each step of the way and what lessons Joseph would need to prepare him for his future task as ruler in Egypt. Potiphar's wife probably thought that she had effectively destroyed Joseph for scorning her advances, but God knew that Joseph needed to be in prison at that particular moment.

Years later, Joseph could look back on his brothers' treachery and declare that they meant it for evil, but God had intended it for good. God's good plans for our lives cannot be thwarted by the evil intentions of others. "If God is for us, who can be against us?" (Romans 8:31).

We do have the freedom to choose whether or not to obey. We have touched on this principle in previous studies, but the truth is that God will never change an individual's personality or make it so that he cannot sin. To do so would be to remove free will, and without free will there can be no meaningful relationship between the Creator and His creation. So God gives us the ability to choose whether we will do what He says—to obey Him—or go our own way.

We see this principle at work even at the time of Creation. In the Garden of Eden, God had told Adam that eating a certain fruit would bring death into the world (see Genesis 2:16–17). However, He did not prevent Adam from eating that fruit. In His sovereign will, He had already made plans to redeem mankind from sin and death, but He still permitted Adam to choose for himself whether or not to obey.

We may not consciously be trying to circumvent the Lord's plan for our lives, but that is exactly what we are doing whenever we deliberately disobey His Word. God's plan cannot be thwarted, and we only hurt ourselves when we disobey. But we enable His fullest blessings in our lives whenever we submissively cooperate with His work.

REFLECTING ON THE TEXT

5) If you were to choose one of the blessings on Jacob's sons, which would it be? Why?

_____

_____

_____

_____

6) In what ways did God show His grace and mercy through the blessings on Jacob's sons? How did He show His justice?

_____

_____

_____

_____

7) When have you, like Joseph, experienced a time of suffering that seemed completely random? How did God show you He was in sovereign control?

_____

_____

_____

8) When has another person done something deliberately evil to you? How did God use that for His glory?

_____

_____

_____

PERSONAL RESPONSE

9) What is God doing in your life today under His sovereign plan? In what ways are you cooperating with Him or fighting against Him?

_____

_____

_____

10) In what areas of your life are you making obedient choices that glorify God? In what areas do your choices need to change?

_____

_____

_____

12

REVIEWING KEY PRINCIPLES

DRAWING NEAR

As you look back at each of the studies in Genesis 34–50, what is the one thing that stood out to you most? What is one new perspective you have learned?

_____

_____

_____

THE CONTEXT

In the preceding studies, we have looked at the family of Jacob and have seen both great weaknesses and great strengths. The characters we have examined were real people, just like us, who were confronted with life in a sinful world. Some of them remained steadfast through it all and faithful to the God they served. Others responded to their circumstances with sinful self-interest. But God worked in the life of each, no matter what his response.

Throughout these studies, we have seen a constant theme: God's sovereignty. We have learned that man does have freedom to choose obedience or disobedience, but no matter what his choice, God remains sovereign. Sometimes His people made terrible choices—actions that led to heartache and even disgrace. Yet every step of the way, God proved His faithfulness to His people, extending grace and reconciliation even to those who had committed terrible sins.

God wants to be reconciled with sinful people, and He commands His people to be reconciled with one another. A key element in this process is to remember that God is sovereign and controls every circumstance in our lives. So even if we are hurt by others, God remains in control and can, in fact, use our pain to make us better people.

Here are a few of the major themes we have found in our study of Jacob and his family. There are many more that we don't have room to reiterate, so take some time to review the earlier studies—or, better still, to meditate on the passages in Scripture that we have covered. Ask the Holy Spirit to give you wisdom and insight into His Word. He will not refuse.

EXPLORING THE MEANING

Vengeance belongs to God, not to us. At the beginning of this study, we saw how Shechem's sin against Dinah brought disgrace on her entire family. Her brothers were right to be angry, but they were wrong to take revenge on the people of that city. By doing so, they were as guilty as Shechem for not controlling their own passions.

We all suffer at the hands of other people from time to time, and sometimes we are called to suffer greatly. We must remember to view such sufferings as God's tools of purification and strengthening for us. Those who hate us are not permitted to cause evil in our lives unless God allows it—and when He does allow it, it is for a reason.

God's reasons for allowing His children to suffer are always intended to bring glory to His name. It may be that He is working to bring the wrongdoer to salvation, or perhaps He is simply making us more like Christ. Whether we can see a reason or not, we must never repay evil with evil. "Beloved, do not avenge yourselves, but rather give place to wrath; for it is written, 'Vengeance is Mine, I will repay,' says the Lord . . . Do not be overcome by evil, but overcome evil with good" (Romans 12:19, 21).

Do not try to simply endure strong temptation—run away! Joseph was a healthy young man in his prime, cut off from family and friends and lonely in a foreign land. As such, the temptations of Potiphar's wife must have been powerful. Yet Joseph demonstrated the right way to deal with such temptations: he fled!

Joseph refused to discuss the subject with the one who tempted him—and refused even to be in her company. In fact, he evidently made a point of trying never to be alone in the house with her. When he did end up alone in her presence, it was by accident. What did he do in this dangerous predicament? He ran away—quite literally, even to the point of leaving his cloak in her hands.

Some situations require us to persevere in daily decisions to please our Father, but others can only be overcome by running away. "Be sober, be vigilant; because your adversary the devil walks about like a roaring lion, seeking whom he may devour. Resist him, steadfast in the faith, knowing that the same sufferings are experienced by your brotherhood in the world" (1 Peter 5:8–9). Sometimes, the best way to resist a roaring lion is to flee.

The Lord uses trials to prepare us for greater tasks. Joseph suffered greatly when his brothers betrayed him, and later when Potiphar's wife falsely accused him. Yet God *permitted* these trials, even though it might have been hard for Joseph to see God's hand at the time. The Lord was, in fact, using those trials to strengthen Joseph's faith and also to teach him practical lessons that he would need later. Joseph had no idea he would one day rule over all Egypt, and he could not have prepared himself with the skills that would be required. Only the Lord knew those things, and He used disappointments, setbacks, slavery, and imprisonment to train Joseph for the future.

We may never become world leaders in this life, but the Lord's plans for our future are still important in the eternal scheme. The day will come when all His people shall rule the world—in fact, we will rule with Him over all creation, for all eternity. He is preparing each of us now to be ready for that great role of leadership, and He uses every circumstance in our lives for that preparation—including suffering and hardship.

Whatever the Lord gives you to do, do it with all your might. Joseph demonstrated this principle by carrying out every task with vigor and diligence. Of course, most of us will never rise to be second in command of a powerful nation as he did. But then again, neither will most of us languish in prison for years under a false accusation.

What is important for us to see is that in both of these positions, Joseph carried out his work with all his might. This is an excellent example of what the Lord calls His people to do. Whatever job He gives us, we are to do it with the attitude that we are serving God directly, rather than men.

"Whatever your hand finds to do, do it with your might; for there is no work or device or knowledge or wisdom in the grave where you are going" (Ecclesiastes 9:10). "And whatever you do, do it heartily, as to the Lord and not to men, knowing that from the Lord you will receive the reward of the inheritance; for you serve the Lord Christ" (Colossians 3:23–24).

The Lord always provides for His people. The famine and drought in Egypt and Canaan were severe, and it is likely that many people died during that time. Yet Jacob's entire household survived. In fact, they did more than just survive—they actually *thrived* while the world around them was in want.

That famine did not catch God by surprise. He ordained it as part of His plan to move Israel into Egypt in preparation for their exodus into the Promised Land of Canaan. He saw all things that would transpire in the future, even to the end of time, and He had planned from before the beginning of time exactly how He would prove His faithfulness to His people.

Sometimes, however, His provision required some of His people to suffer. Joseph suffered grievously prior to being elevated to the leadership of Egypt, and it is likely that he wondered at times whether God had forgotten him. But the Lord had not forgotten Joseph, or any others in the family of Israel, and He proved His faithfulness by providing for all their needs. He never forgets His promises or His children.

God's people should always be reconciled with one another. Joseph never showed any inclination to get revenge on his brothers, or on anyone else who wronged him. His desire was just the opposite: to be reunited in unity and love with his family. The moment he had an opportunity, he set about working toward that reconciliation.

This is the example for all of God's people. We are to make reconciliation and forgiveness a top priority in our lives. People do sin, and sometimes they will hurt us—deliberately or not, the pain is the same. Our job in such circumstances is to approach the person who has offended us—not to confront him with his sin but to offer forgiveness and reconciliation. This principle works in both directions—whether we are the offended or the ones who gave offense.

"Therefore if you bring your gift to the altar, and there remember that your brother has something against you, leave your gift there before the altar, and go your way. First be reconciled to your brother, and then come and offer your gift" (Matthew 5:23–24).

God is in control of all our circumstances, even when things seem to be going wrong. This is the overarching theme of these events in Genesis. The Lord had told Abraham, many years before Joseph was born, that his descendants would go into Egypt for 400 years (see Genesis 15:13–14). It was His plan from the beginning that Joseph should lead his family into Egypt, and the events we covered in these studies were part of that plan.

But the hand of God was not readily apparent in these situations, particularly to the people who were living through them. Joseph probably did not sit rejoicing at the bottom of the pit, thrilled that God was sending him to Egypt to fulfill His prophecy to Abraham. It is much more likely that he was overcome with grief and fear, wondering what was going to happen next—wondering, indeed, whether or not his own brothers would murder him.

Yet the Lord is completely sovereign over all things in our lives, and He has promised that He will always be faithful to His children. "And we know that all things work together for good to those who love God, to those who are the called according to His purpose" (Romans 8:28).

We are still responsible for our own actions. The other side to the previous principle is that God's sovereignty does not exonerate us from our own responsibility. Joseph's brothers were fully responsible before God for attempting to murder him and for selling him into slavery.

The Lord can and does use the wicked actions of evil men to accomplish His holy purposes, because His plans cannot be thwarted by the conduct of human beings or even by Satan himself. But this is to the glory of God, not to the praise of wicked men. Joseph's brothers still had to answer for their deeds, even though God used those deeds to further His plans for Israel.

The good news is that the Lord also uses our obedience to further His purposes and bring glory to His name—and we grow in Christlikeness in the process. Joseph's responses to his brothers' deeds demonstrated this, and his life became a picture of the life of Christ.

Unleashing the Text

1) Which of the concepts or principles in this study have you found to be the most encouraging? Why?

_____

_____

_____

_____

2) Which of the concepts or principles have you found most challenging? Why?

_____

_____

_____

_____

3) What aspects of "walking with God" are you already doing in your life? Which areas need strengthening?

_____

_____

_____

_____

4) To which of the main characters that we've studied have you most been able to relate? How might you emulate that person in your own life?

_____

_____

_____

PERSONAL RESPONSE

5) Have you taken a definite stand for Jesus Christ? Have you accepted His free gift of salvation? If not, what is preventing you from doing so?

_____

_____

_____

6) In what areas of your life have you been most convicted during this study? What exact things will you do to act upon these convictions? Be specific.

_____

_____

_____

7) What have you learned about the character of God during this study? How has this insight affected your worship or prayer life?

_____

_____

_____

8) What are some specific things that you want to see God do in your life in the coming month? What are some things that you intend to change in your own life during that time? (Return to this list in one month and hold yourself accountable to fulfill these things.)

_____

_____

_____

If you would like to continue in your study of the Old Testament, read the next title in this series: *Exodus and Numbers: The Exodus from Egypt.*

ALSO AVAILABLE

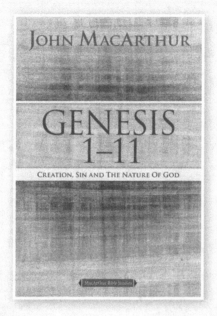

In this study, John MacArthur guides readers through an in-depth look at the creation story, the first murder, Noah and the Flood, the first covenant, the Tower of Babel, and the dispersion of the nations. This study includes close-up examinations of Adam, Eve, Cain, Abel, and Noah, as well as careful considerations of doctrinal themes such as "The Fall of Man" and "Heritage and Family."

The MacArthur Bible Studies provide intriguing examinations of the whole of Scripture. Each guide incorporates extensive commentary, detailed observations on overriding themes, and probing questions to help you study the Word of God with guidance from John MacArthur.

ALSO AVAILABLE

I n this study, John MacArthur guides readers through an in-depth look at the historical period beginning with Abraham's call from God, continuing through his relocation in the land of Canaan, and concluding with the story of his grandsons Jacob and Esau. This study includes close-up examinations of Sarah, Hagar, Ishmael, and Isaac, as well as careful considerations of doctrinal themes such as "Covenant and Obedience" and "Wrestling with God."

The MacArthur Bible Studies provide intriguing examinations of the whole of Scripture. Each guide incorporates extensive commentary, detailed observations on overriding themes, and probing questions to help you study the Word of God with guidance from John MacArthur.

ALSO AVAILABLE

In this study, John MacArthur guides readers through an in-depth look at the historical period beginning with God's calling of Moses, continuing through the giving of the Ten Commandments, and concluding with the Israelites' preparations to enter the Promised Land. This study includes close-up examinations of Aaron, Caleb, Joshua, Balaam and Balak, as well as careful considerations of doctrinal themes such as "Complaints and Rebellion" and "Following God's Law."

The MacArthur Bible Studies provide intriguing examinations of the whole of Scripture. Each guide incorporates extensive commentary, detailed observations on overriding themes, and probing questions to help you study the Word of God with guidance from John MacArthur.